# Chevy
## at the
# Levee

D R E A M S

LOU GALLIO

# Contents

*In loving memory of my wife Pat; and dedicated to Peter and Angela, our beautiful children, with great admiration, pride and love. And to our extended family in America, the United Kingdom and Canada.*

# Acknowledgments

To medical professionals, caregivers and clergy who passionately tend to the aged, the sick and oppressed; may God bless you. A special thanks to Burt and Laneda for the use of their beach house and to my editor, Gary Hassig, for his meticulous, professional work.

# Disclaimer

This book reflects the author's recollection of people, places and events spanning many years. Other than dialogue and circumstances as best remembered, the author changed some names, characteristics and conditions to protect the privacy of those involved.

# Preface

I thought I would die before my wife. I was wrong. This book relates to those who have lost loved ones and those who will face grief. It also aims to entertain life's brighter side, the happy days, the good times. The story begins in the 50s, with a lifetime of amusement, romance, adventure and drama. Then came loss, trauma and unusual grief dreams. As words of poignant emotions edged into this story, it was cathartic with a speck of personal relief. Hopefully, readers will gain insight and value in this experience.

# Chapter One

## Beginning of the End

My wife rushed towards the boarding ramp; suddenly, she stopped, turned to me and burst out crying. Unlike Pat's usual wave and a broad smile, it was a troubled face and teardrops at the San Francisco Airport. She pirouetted and faded inside the dark boarding tunnel and the airline agent slammed the door shut. I stood rooted in place, rigid in shock. My heart dropped to my knees and my eyes welled up in tears.

Pat was usually upbeat, gregarious and under control. She seldom cried unless in the grip of intense emotions. Like on the transatlantic flight to America when she first left her home in England. This time, the airport episode again flared her feelings, but the reason was different. A week later, she was diagnosed with deadly brain cancer. "Glioblastoma multiforme" is a frightening term and its diabolical course is dreadful.

The airport episode was a surprising, traumatic end to an otherwise enjoyable retreat together. I was on contract with an internet company in Emeryville, California, on the East Bay across San Francisco. Pat stayed in Dallas during that time, so we were apart except for short visits. Consequently, I was not aware of the onset of Pat's disease. She had seemed to enjoy the time at the apartment in Emeryville. Freshly equipped with new, comfortable furniture and enveloped by a marina near the east end of the Bay Bridge, it was an ideal place for Pat's vacation and private time.

"This is nice! The bay, a Trader Vic's within walking distance," Pat cooed as she set foot in the apartment a few days earlier. It was an opportunity to enhance our relationship and renew courtship in a refreshingly different scenario away from our humdrum routines. It felt like our beginning in London when we were courting, falling in love.

Amid pleasant memories, I hate thinking about that painful experience at the airport—it has forever seared my mind. I try to ease the pain with thoughts about our courtship, sincere love, romance, family and the good times we shared. By all accounts, we had a wonderful life together. Nonetheless, the dark days remain like an ominous shadow and the agony lingers. Anyone who has dealt with a similar experience—especially about a loved one—feels its heart-wrenching effects and permanency of grief.

Today, I'm sitting on the sun deck of a beach house on Crystal Beach, Texas, contemplating writing my story many years later. It's a perfect place for kicking back, taking in the best of the Texas coast and gathering my thoughts. This pleasant Tuesday morning, the radiant sun glitters brightly, reflecting off the line of cascading waves. The weekend beach raiders have vacated and returned to their homes in surrounding communities or hotels nearby.

Meanwhile, the Gulf of Mexico's current undulates its pearl-crested waves that sweep the mauve-pink sand—a placating, hypnotic white noise pleasing to the ears. I plunge deeper into the far reaches of memory. The ambiance of a misty breeze blowing across my face under the Texas sun stimulates nostalgia. My mind begins to unfold the past.

Some memories are like exquisite, glistening jewelry in a box. Such as when I first saw Pat striding down the London Embassy hallway in front of a group of Marine Guards (I was one of them). Her head down, she blushed in embarrassment; her stiletto heels clicked quick-time on the marble-slabbed floor. Then there was the time when we first met. It was by chance, face-to-face in the embassy doorway. And later, having lunch together in Grosvenor Square was an absolute delight. I enjoyed how Pat savored the sight and aromatic scent of the beautiful flower garden in the park.

I'm smiling broadly now.

I recall the days of strolling the streets of London with Pat. We went to jazz clubs in Soho, concerts at the Palladium, espresso shops and touristy places. Often, we would stop at a fish and chips shop or buy roasted chestnuts from street vendors. After my guard duty on liberty weekends, we would rush to take an Austin Black Cab to St. Pancras train station and board a steam locomotive I nicknamed "Beetle-Bomb." We sat in its vintage cabins on velvety burgundy seats looking out the broad window, watching the scenic landscape slide past. The train chugged towards Corby, some 100 miles north of London to visit her family. I enjoyed going to the open market to shop in the town square on Saturday mornings in Corby. I usually had a break-fast of bacon, eggs, beans, mushrooms, tomatoes, pork sausage and "black pudding," a type of blood sausage. On Saturday afternoons, Pat's dad Albert and I would sip Johnny Walker Black and watch sports on the "telly," trying to avoid the eyesight of Pat and her mother, Lovey, a name short for "Lovina."

We visited relatives in Aberdeen, Scotland, Pat's birthplace—a beautiful area bordering the North Sea. We sometimes navigated meandering dirt roads in the Highlands near or in the clouds, delighting in the fresh air amid the heather's purple hue—another treasured memory jewel.

And later in our lives, I can visualize Pat on the pier near my apartment in Emeryville stretched out on a lawn recliner reading a novel. She was a prolific reader and it thrilled me to know she was in her element, enjoying it immensely. While Pat savored a book on a bright sunny day, a gentle breeze whisked through her silky auburn hair and smiling face.

Another jewel in the box, albeit a slightly sad one: our parting after my tour of duty in London was over. Clad in a heavy woolen overcoat, Pat stood on a snow-blanketed train platform in Corby, waving goodbye amid falling snowflakes, as Beetle-Bomb began chugging down the tracks to London. Our two-year courtship in the U.K. was sadly interrupted. When I made it back to the States, I immediately proposed marriage by phone, and she was to join me in America when my time was up in the Marines.

Then tragedy struck.

Before Pat was to leave for America, she was in a car accident and suffered significant injuries. I flew back to England to stay with her. Being a resilient Scottish lassie, after several months she steadily recovered and we flew to America together.

I pause my cogitating momentarily to survey the expanse of Crystal Beach again. I notice a woman in a bikini pulling a red wagon with two small kids inside: a girl and a boy. It reminds me of my red Radio Flyer wagon as a youngster. I used the wagon and a scale to sell Dad's juicy tomatoes for fifteen cents a pound. Mom, a first-generation Italian-American and Dad, a direct Sicilian immigrant, kept a quarter-acre garden where we lived in Pear Ridge, a rural part of Port Arthur, Texas. Besides Dad's garden, we had a cow, chickens, two giant pecan trees and a half-dozen fruit trees. As far as food, we were reasonably self-sufficient only buying flour, sugar, condiments, cold cuts and a pork roast for our traditional spaghetti dinner on Sundays.

People-watching, bird-watching, and sunbathing stimulate an intimate release for reflection while at the beach. I think about the many crazy times my close friend, Lucian "Bo" Guilbeau, and I had at McFaddin Beach, about a mile away. Bo was a classmate and more like a brother. We would swim, sunbathe on the beach, hang out all day and depending on how much money we had, buy a burger and fries at the Breeze Inn, a nondescript restaurant bar. The place was a rustic cedarwood bijou structure perched high on pilings protruding from the beach like most in hurricane zones.

At the beach house where I'm staying, a sign on a wall says, "*The Sea Called My Soul and I Answered with All My Heart.*" How true that is. At this moment on the sun deck, the circumstances couldn't be better: a cup of bold *Seaport* coffee, the brand Dad used in his old-fashioned aluminum drip pot and a fresh, soothing breeze. I watch a swarm of playful swallows chirping, fluttering around a cluster of gourd nests hung on a galvanized pipe, stuck in the berm that rims the beach. The sky is a mosaic of scattered, thin layers of misty stratus clouds. The subtle, soothing sound of waves crashing on the beach is hypnotic. Sometimes, the sun peeks through the occlusion and winks; perhaps it's God's way of watching, warming the soul and hopefully, casting His grace and light. I often think Pat is shining her light too! I tilt my head back, fix my gaze through and beyond the haze and wonder, *Is Pat looking down at me?* I'm mesmerized, a hopeless sentimentalist.

I pause to sip my coffee and scan the horizon, across the bay towards Galveston Island, where I boarded the ferry just yesterday. Waiting for the vessel was calmer than the frantic tourist weekends on the Gulf coast but monotonous. Once on the boat, I leaned on the bulkhead railing, enjoying the brisk 25-knot wind in my face. I watched a pair of dolphins oscillating in and out of the water and a flock of cawing seagulls—Black Skimmers—on the search for prey. The setting reminded me of Pat when we courted in Texas, frolicking at the beach and lounging on the levee in Port Arthur.

It's the same choppy water, the same coastline, the same soothing breeze—the same eternalized scene—our Chevy at the levee and having a picnic with Pat.

Now, on with the story.

# Chapter Two

## Bewilderment

Every time I recall that fateful day at the San Francisco airport, I slip into a state of malaise—physically, emotionally, spiritually—in a mood of dysphoria, hopelessness. Grief is omnipresent. It also accents the loving characteristics of a lost one, and with Pat, there are many. She was always a joyful person. Always. She was never sad, timid or careless, especially when leaving on a flight back home. I had no clue what the problem was, little chance to reach her, embrace her, help in her mysterious demise. I figured Pat's send-off at the airport would be routine. Far from it. The entire incident took me by surprise. When she entered the ramp tunnel, my mind, my spirit emptied. The sight of her in that condition pierced my very soul.

I can hardly describe the traumatic effects during that scene, apart from becoming anxious and slipping into despair. Sometimes when I think about it, I become listless, lackluster in attitude with a touch of suspended animation. I try to avoid this condition, but I suffer its terrible, devastating effects. But in retrospect, on that day she *was* acting peculiar, disoriented and confused during our trip to the airport. I should've guessed something was wrong. Maneuvering our way through the traffic in my classic sedan, I noticed Pat had an odd, distant look in her eyes. Even worse, she was silent and withdrawn, which puzzled me further since she was a conversationalist. She seemed fine at the apartment when we were making ready to leave but became silent on the way to the airport.

Pat typically started most of our one-on-one interactions. I was the quiet one in our partnership, often needing prodding for conversation. In contrast, Pat was a consummate talker with a cute accent, a slight Scottish intonation derived from growing to ten years in Aberdeen. I always depended on Pat's special communicative skills to start cheerful conversations, to set the environmental tone. After all, she was a professional telephone operator specially trained by a vocational school in London. She had the perfect voice, an energetic presence, a magical elixir that made people attracted to her, like her, trust her. Pat was an expert at appeasing customers and for that matter, anyone in her presence.

Even before we left for the airport that day, I was bothered by her solitude. I wanted her to get back to her usual upbeat self. I began conversations to prime her chatty nature, but her tepid responsiveness should have been my wake-up call. On impulse and to root out her issue, I initiated a conversation about her stay at the apartment in Emeryville.

As another diversion, I discussed a trivial topic about how we might change our condo's interior design in Dallas. I hated bringing up such a mundane subject with random questions, but I needed to do something. I had to know Pat was okay and the only way I could carry this out was to hear her voice, analyze her state of mind. Unfortunately, it didn't draw any hints. Pat gave me an endearing grin as if she knew it was a ploy.

She said rather glibly, "Let's think about it and decide later."

She continued basking in her silence and judging from her seemingly innocent answer, her reaction, her smile. My mood went from anxious to contentment. As though everything was in order. I presumed Pat's depressive mood was mainly because of her over-thinking her trip back home. I thought maybe Pat was pondering her flight and the treadmill routine in Dallas. Had I any idea of an issue, I would have convinced her to stay longer to relax and relieve her mind from whatever worries. Instead, we continued our way to the airport with taciturn Pat.

Even the unusually serene and carefree ambiance of traveling the freeway wasn't enough to convince her to discuss any problems freely. She just sat quietly in the passenger seat, observing the land-scape, a line of fleeting Eucalyptus trees. Her silence was also alarming because we never felt the need to hide anything. We openly shared everything in our lives had no secrets between us. I knew about Pat's life long before we came under wedlock and the same with her. She knew about my life. Pat's behavior was perplexing and I tried my utmost to find the cause of her discomfort, her sad state of mind.

As we neared the airport, my concern became more intense. Even if Pat had given me her traditional *"I'm okay, don't worry"* smirk, it wouldn't have put an end to my quest. Within a few minutes, I began another conversation with small talk.

"Looks like we might get some rain today."

I felt silly saying it, but it *was* overcast at the time, with a reasonable number of low clouds about to reach the road. Though this was normal for the Bay area, I tried to engage her somehow, urge her to give me a clue why she was so mired in melancholy.

"Hope not. Might delay the flight." Pat said, rather casually, with a blank stare fixed straight ahead.

My efforts to cheer her up were persistent, but I couldn't change her sad demeanor. Pat answered my questions with diversionary platitudes and a continual stare at the road as if to reflect upon an issue or circumstance. Every time I probed for reasons behind her behavior, she scoffed and brushed it off.

"Lou, you worry too much. Everything is fine, just fine." She would say in an even tone, her voice trailing off.

Her mannerisms, lack of eye contact and isolation were most disturbing. She had never acted this way before.

I responded, "Well, okay, Sweetie. If you say so." I had no choice but to back off, allow her to bask in her silence and continue driving steadily.

Exasperated, I tightened my grip on the steering wheel. We had to reach the airport before check-in time. Otherwise, Pat might be late and she didn't like being late. Being late would have not only disrupted her schedule but would be an added blow to her state of mind. I was willing to do whatever it took to arrive at the airport on time in a safe manner.

I carefully accelerated our speed towards the airport and used every driving skill I had garnered over the years to avoid any mishaps. Because of her car accident years before, Pat was somewhat skittish about being on the road. But instead of her usual anxiety and my show of urgency, she showed no signs of apprehension. She was apathetic, continuing with her brooding, showing no concern about what was transpiring.

Seemingly, all she cared about was some issue, which inexplicably engulfed her. Most disturbing, Pat was unable or unwilling to describe her predicament. She kept it compartmentalized inside. I could see it was negatively affecting her psyche. Pat was always a lively, optimistic person who rarely hid her feelings for extended periods, if at all. I sensed something had to change her disposition before running the risk of suffering from an acute ailment. At my wit's end, my anxiety level was quickly rising. I grappled for answers to why this was happening. Maybe it was because her tranquil stay in California had ended, which was an acceptable, anticlimactic reaction. This analysis offered a bit of relief, but I wasn't sure it was altogether correct. I had hoped once she was at the airport, ready to board the airplane, the dark cloud of depression would lift and she would return to her bubbly self.

Momentarily reflecting on positive thoughts, I shifted my focus on getting to the airport early. I considered possible shortcuts. I managed to enter the overpass and began cruising towards the airport at a pretty good clip. Within minutes, we had finally reached the airport. After parking the car, we gathered luggage and steadily headed towards the gate. As it turns out, there was a slight delay in the flight. My efforts to rush were unnecessary, but the extra time might help Pat pull out of her strange mood. We sat in the waiting area discussing her visit and by all counts, she thoroughly enjoyed herself. Gradually, she began reverting to her usual disposition. It calmed my nerves, but more importantly, Pat appeared to be getting back to normal. And she would not feel any more discomfort.

Suddenly, she fidgeted, twitched her head, stood and said, "I'm going to the lady's room and look in some shops. I won't be long."

I was suspect, hesitant to let her go alone, but agreed anyway.

"Make it quick, Sweetie. They'll be boarding soon."

She strolled towards the multi-colored array of neon signs, shops and restaurants. Window shopping wasn't unusual and Pat was seldom late for anything, especially a long flight back home.

After she left, I stood, walked away, and looked through a stretch of ceiling-to-floor plate-glass windows to make my systematic assessment of the weather. It was partly cloudy with a pleasant 63 degrees, the same as in Emeryville, across the Bay Bridge where my apartment was. I noticed a gentle Pacific breeze pushing through a laggard cluster of cotton-ball clouds. The puffy nimbus aerosols had grey underbellies and were drifting listlessly overhead with a threat of rain. Instead, only a drizzle fell, typical for the Bay area.

Then an airline agent announced, "Now pre-boarding for Dallas."

The agent's voice echoed all over, practically reaching every corner of the expansive terminal. I scanned the area. No sign of Pat yet. I continued my gaze out the window, watching aircraft taking off and landing, reminiscent of my days of flying private airplanes for business and pleasure.

After a considerable time, the airline agent announced the Dallas flight again. "Dallas flight boarding shortly." The agent explained how to line up in front of the check-in counter when she broadcasted the start of boarding. Boarding passes in hands, a swarm of impatient people rushed to the snaky line anyway and jostled for a place. The chatter increased along with the clamor, which in turn heightened my acute sense of urgency. It prompted me to pivot and set my sights on where Pat and I were sitting. The seats were empty.

Then I turned in every direction, searching for a glimpse of her. She was nowhere in sight.

The scenario slowly sent a shock down my spine. I began checking all the passengers one by one as they jammed in line and streamed towards the boarding gate.

The agent announced, "Boarding for Dallas," further stating the flight number.

Passengers immediately started moving towards the counter, showing their passes, checking in and entering the boarding bridge. Pat was not in line. To be sure, I looked down the tunnel ramp leading to the plane's fore cabin portal, where a flight attendant stood greeting travelers. Pat was not there. Of course not. She would not have left without saying goodbye. I checked the crowd in the terminal again, the surrounding area and other locations. A sudden sense of great concern struck.

Tormenting minutes ticked away as the boarding line dwindled and travelers disappeared through the portal—still no trace of Pat. At this point, it was cause for grave concern. My mind swirled with unnerving, gloomy thoughts. But I managed to shake it off and continued my search. I had to suck it up, find Pat and help her board the plane. My mind strayed, reviewing her brief stay and what could have driven her to act so strangely, so withdrawn. I had no clue. In my view, she enjoyed her visit with no apparent issues.

Pat came to Emeryville for a brief vacation while on contract with an Internet company. Emeryville is a small town, a bedroom community, on the East Bay across San Francisco at the Bay Bridge's foot on Oakland and Berkeley's corridor. Enveloped by a marina, my apartment complex was absent from the city's hustle-bustle, an ideal place for Pat's vacation away from self-imposed responsibilities.

During her visit, Pat was a bit reserved. But by all indications, nothing was wrong. She had immersed herself in solitude. Maybe I should have inquired about her sad demeanor but chalked it up to jet lag, rest and relaxation. She was relishing a well-deserved break away from her routine. As a dedicated worker, she didn't have much time off. She never shunned her domestic chores either; she was very family-oriented, like her family in the U.K.

Even when our kids, Peter and Angela, were in school, she worked for the school district so she would be home when school was out and vice versa. By the time Peter and Angela went to college, we both had two jobs: she worked as a secretary at a bank during the day and a hotel telephone operator in the evening. My day job was with an Internet company and a retail computer store on evenings and weekends. When I began traveling, she shirked idle time at home and continued working. She thoroughly enjoyed interacting and social-izing in a work setting.

But she also looked forward to the trip to California, a much-deserved vacation. The visit was primarily for relaxation and a self-imposed work schedule break. Her inherent work ethic matched those of her parents, who were hard workers in the U.K.

My apartment was a perfect get-away nestled on a small peninsula surrounded by a marina overlooking the Bay. The second-story, upscale flat offered an ideal view of the marina cove on both sides. The windows framed the water, the boats bobbing to the rhythm of gentle waves and a long pier extending out. It was a tranquil, isolated situation, yet conveniently near stores and entertainment centers. It was in a unique setting. We had easy access to shops and entertain-ment with little road traffic, though surrounded by water.

When Pat first saw the apartment, her face beamed and she said, "I love it!"

Her response was inspiring. The temporary separation magically offered some perquisites, a refreshing rendezvous. It was an opportu-nity to revitalize our marital commitment to one another. It gave both of us brief privacy and independence, then reconfirmed our unabated love as it was in London.

Pat again succumbed to her pragmatic ways when she asked, "This place is amazing. It must cost a lot. You know, I would've enjoyed the studio flat too."

I replied, "Yeah, well, rent is expensive, but it's worth it. Take a good look." I pointed out the window at the long dock, the body of water below.

Pat peered through the window and said, "Fantastic!"

She gaped at the marina, the pier ending with a rounded nook and the tranquil cove. The layout was remarkably accommodating. The wooden platform spanned about thirty yards over the marina basin, far enough to allow blissful solitude. Occasionally, an airliner or small plane buzzed overhead, along with squeals of seagulls. It was perfect for Pat's favorite pastime setting, other than merely reading a book. Add serenity and perhaps self-reflection lounging on the pier, and it would become one of my favorite pastimes as well.

I can still visualize Pat on the pier, stretched out on a lawn recliner reading a novel. Reading was routine for her, particularly at bedtime. In this case, she had the luxury of personal time in an exotic setting. It pleased me to know she was in her element, immensely enjoying it. One scene stood out: the rush of wind caressing Pat's face on a bright, sunny day. The gentle breeze whisked through her stylishly coiffed, silky auburn hair and brushed across her creamy white, squarish face. Her eyes simultaneously radiated intuitive awareness, empathy and optimism. Her soft lips paired well with a cute button nose that often itched. Pat habitually rubbed her nose with the knuckle of her index finger. Not having allergies, her itching may have been linked with superstitions like *someone loves you or needs you*, or *you're about to have a visitor or receive money*.

These intricacies were Pat's world. She was a quintessential extrovert who loved people. She was popular among all who knew her and they reciprocated with unconditional love for her. She was also fortunate with gaming and had remarkable intuition and a hint of extrasensory perception. Together with this, Pat was intelligent and quick to laugh. She always wore a grin, accompanied by a glow in her eyes, signaling spontaneous empathy. Her presence and positive attitude were contagious. Looking at her made you smile in an instant. When she walked into a room, she lit it up with light straight from her heart. Her heart instantly emanated her identity, her persona. She had a sunny, sparkling presence about her.

I vowed to make sure her smile never faded. Even if it meant relinquishing my ego or sense of self, I was ready to make the sacrifice.

Lucky for us, we never reached that point. Our relationship stood the test of time. We always solved every problem together before the issue had reared its ugly head at the airport.

Pat was only five foot three yet graciously carried herself every step of the way. She was also a fantastic singer with a rich, melodic voice, a supple dancer, athlete and an avid sports fan. She was a Scottish lassie of outstanding stock, roots in Carr and Marshall families in Aberdeen, northeast Scotland. Her dad hailed from Clan Campbell, one of the most prominent families of the Highlands. Pat's maternal side, the Clan Carr (Kerr) of Norse influence, was loyal and warlike on the turbulent Scottish Borders. It wasn't Pat's personal choice as the clan system spread across Scotland from the Highlands many centuries ago when several countries invaded Scotland. As a result, it became a mixing bowl of cultures. Pat inherited all the positive traits, such as being fun-loving, down-to-earth, honest, hard-working and loyal. She was also fair, austere, fiery and bold. To me, she was a beautiful gem, firm in her beliefs.

During her visit, I had perceived her demeanor as utter relaxation and a transcendent state. The reason for this was quite simple; Pat had rarely succumbed to these environments. She would rather spend time working, but while on her visit, it seemed she had submerged herself entirely with nature. And I wanted to enjoy these moments with her. On the surface, she looked happy and content with our time together. But despite Pat's otherwise enjoyable vacation, the situation slowly transformed into horror.

# Chapter Three

## The Nightmare

I t seemed an eternity had passed since Pat had gone missing, wandering somewhere in the airport. The numbness I experienced in my failed search for her took a heavy toll. I felt suspended in limbo. Pat had never done this before. The episode had sucked the energy out of my body. My worry would only subside when I saw Pat's smiling face again.

All kinds of imaginings cluttered my mind. When I sat down to catch my breath, people turned and gave me curious looks. I soon realized my ashen face and anxiety must've been a strange sight. Then, an elderly couple stopped and inquired about my predicament.

The man asked, "Excuse me, sir. You look upset. What's the matter? Are you ill?"

Normally I would dismiss strangers approaching me, a defensive mechanism acquired over time in a war zone and other dangerous places. But this time, the man was benevolent, warmly compassionate. I felt I could air my feelings. My mind racing, I had difficulty explaining my dilemma—too many questions, too many "what ifs" to consider. I forced myself to utter at least something in response.

"My wife, she's lost somewhere in the terminal. Can't find her."

Their faces went compassionate. They absorbed the trauma of my situation.

The man said, "Lost in the airport? Things like that happen in a place like this. But no need to worry yourself sick." He paused. "Can we help?"

It was a wake-up call to get a grip, think straight, develop a plan of action. Taking a deep breath, I shook my head and responded.

"Oh, no. No thanks. She'll show up soon, or I'll find her eventually."

"Are you sure we can't help?"

"Yes, I'm sure. Thanks anyway. It'll be okay. It's just that this has never happened before." I straightened my posture and looked away to end the conversation.

The man persisted. "Well, try to relax, give yourself a break. It's easy to think the worst, but things will work out. Did you have the ticket agent announce her name over the loudspeaker?"

"Well, no, I haven't."

The conversation gave me a renewed glimmer of hope to continue the quest to find my Pat. I quickly thanked the couple and focused on the task at hand. Pat's long absence still unnerved me; negative thoughts soon began to creep in again, but I quickly shrugged them off. Taking the man's suggestion, I assumed a positive attitude and concentrated on the mission: finding Pat before she missed her flight.

I made my way towards the ticket counter and had the airline agent beckon Pat to the ticket counter. I waited for several minutes, but she didn't show up. Then I quick-stepped towards the row of boutique shops and restaurants for a recheck. Thinking she might have stopped for a soda before the flight and didn't hear the announcement. I went inside an eatery, queried one of the waiters and described Pat's features.

Much to my dismay, he hadn't seen her, but he had just started his shift and pointed to the manager, saying he might know something.

I felt a sudden rush of hope and headed towards the manager. I described Pat again.

The manager shook his head. "No, I haven't seen anyone like her."

His response further heightened my anxiety. I repeated the process with other shops but had no luck. I couldn't afford to waste time, so I rushed back to the boarding area to take another look. Perhaps Pat had returned in the meantime and would be looking for me. Boarding had begun. Passengers were lining up near our flight portal. I quickly scanned the crowd, hoping to spot Pat. Nothing. I went closer to the boarding gate. Maybe I would find her in front of the line, but no sign of her.

I carefully searched the perimeter, the seating area, every corner, but she was nowhere in sight. I felt shrouded by a blanket of doom and darkness. Then I knew her disappearance somehow related to her unusual demeanor. If only she had communicated what was going on, I could have helped her avoid this anomaly. Nonetheless, her condition and current actions had baffled me beyond understanding.

My mind replayed recent events again for clues. On recollection, Pat seemingly had the time of her life during her stay in Emeryville. She was her usual self on the surface, especially when dining with her cousin Michael in San Francisco and later touring the wine country. We had an enjoyable, memorable time together.

But a glut of disturbing possibilities entered my mind. Some so grim, I tried desperately to divert my attention from them. And then, I spontaneously replayed Pat's strange behavior on our way to the airport.

Meanwhile, I saw a man in the terminal carrying a fishing rod during my frantic search. It made me think of another strange event where Pat had shown signs of confusion, a misconception. Maybe there was a connection. The incident had occurred a few weeks earlier in Berkeley, but I could recall every detail. We were having lunch with a friend I had met at a local 1st Marine Division Association meeting. It was a popular restaurant in the middle of town. A favorite of Pat's, it was simple yet clean and comfortable, with a family-style American menu, a pleasant atmosphere and well-prepared food that suited her modest needs. Our table was on the back wall, which butted up against a vacant expanse of land outside. Belying its ordinary appearance, the restaurant had massive panoramic windows large enough to enjoy a broad landscape view. Pat would typically select a spot next to the windows, which provided a serene ambiance where she could enjoy the view. The waiter seated us at her favorite table, the one with the best vantage point. Our gathering was going well up until Pat made a bizarre observation.

Peering out the window, she pointed at an image on the bank of a small reservoir and said, "Look...look over there. The man fishing."

I carefully surveyed the scene. A few feet above the ground, leading to the water, a steel platform straddled the reservoir bank. Attached to the platform was a staircase with hand railings. After repeated efforts, I still couldn't see a fisherman, although, from a skewed viewpoint, it *did* vaguely resemble a man sitting with a fishing pole.

I said, "Sweetie, it's just a platform and a set of stairs."

Our friend looked at the scene and nodded concurrence. Pat hesitated, then turned to me with a quizzical expression. "Are you sure?"

I nodded. "Yes."

She wrinkled her brow and stared at the staircase again. She shook her head, sighed and said, "Guess you're right. I thought maybe, well, never mind."

I gave an appeasing smile and blew it off. "It's okay. That happens to a lot of people."

I told myself it was an anomaly, an illusion, nothing serious. The sparse misinterpretation of sensory information is a harmless aberration. But then Pat glanced at it again and gave a nervous response.

She said, "Have you looked at it closely?"

After hearing Pat's analysis for the second time, my friend and I nodded acknowledgment.

Pat responded, "Oh well."

I tried to comfort her. Turning to my friend, I said, "I'm guessing even our battle-hardened Marine here suffered misperception some time or another. Right?"

"You bet. Even worse! In Nam, I had bizarre visions, hallucinations, especially at night!" His response prompted us all to chuckle, bringing the subject to an end.

But my curiosity and concern lingered. Pat's conclusion was disturbing. After some thought, I recalled reading about "Sensory Processing Disorder," which occurs when sensory information gets mixed up, resulting in various jumbled perceptions in the brain. With this condition, a person's vision becomes distorted, creating odd impressions. Multiple potential causes stem from neurological or physical ailments such as nutrition, sleep apnea, stress, or illness. But why would it happen to Pat? She was the most upbeat person I've ever known.

She hadn't suffered from any mental or physical anomalies, illnesses, or adverse conditions during our time together. And no one among

Pat's relatives or friends had mentioned any previous ailments. Throughout her life, Pat had always been healthy, energetic, athletic, agile and alert. Such an illness was not logical.

Back to the airport debacle. My quest to find Pat became more intense. I again surveyed the cluster of passengers lined up in front of the gateway, continually craning my body and moving to different angles of vision to find her. I consistently rejected the idea that I had lost her, all the while side-stepping, pushing my way through the crowd. She's never missed a flight before. One by one, the line of travelers streamed through check-in and into the boarding tunnel, but not Pat.

The last person passed the counter. A few minutes later, the airline agent announced, "Last call for boarding."

At this point, the tense situation became a potentially disastrous plight. I immediately ran back through the terminal again, zigzagging through the crowded hallway. I swiveled, looking in all directions. On the verge of losing hope, I finally spotted her! She was inside a shop, rummaging through a rack of clothing. Pat appeared utterly oblivious to the impending mishap.

I rushed to her. "Sweetie, I've been looking all over for you. They're boarding the plane now!"

At first, she turned to me, startled and bewildered. A frown crossed her face, but she said nothing. After a pause, she said, "Sorry." A trace of remorse was in her eyes like she had misbehaved.

I took her hand. "We have to hurry."

We swiftly weaved through the crowd and dashed back to the gate. Once we were there, we stopped and faced each other. I placed my hands on Pat's shoulders, looked into her eyes and asked, "Sweetie, what's wrong? What's bothering you?"

She looked at me with a confused stare but managed a slight smile and said, "Nothing."

I angled my head and gave her a look of disbelief. "I've never seen you this way before."

Then Pat lowered her head slightly, shook her head, sighed and uttered, "I don't know."

My throat tightened and I swallowed hard. There was no time to query further. It was decision time. I had to get Pat on the plane. We moved towards check-in. The ticket agent was about to close the ramp door but saw us and motioned us to hurry. We paused, hugged and shared a quick kiss. But I was still alarmed.

I told her, "Sweetie, be sure to call me when you get to Dallas."

With a grin, she nodded and said, "Okay."

In a state of apprehension, I watched her walk briskly towards the boarding portal. As she approached the gate, I stood teary-eyed.

Oddly, at that moment, I spontaneously encapsulated our relationship. Pat meant everything to me. She was my best friend, my confidant, my kindred spirit, my love, the center of my universe. My whole world revolved around her. I would be nothing without her. Before we came together in London, my life was a blur, a rudderless ship meandering from one island to another with no exact destination in mind. After transforming from a teen miscreant to a regimented Marine, I met Pat and we married. That's when my adult life story began. We had a happy, loving relationship and raised two beautiful, successful children.

Our first meeting at the London Embassy was unforgettable. It seemed like yesterday, but it had been some forty-two years earlier. The Marine Corps had brought us together when they sent me to the embassy as a Marine Security Guard. Funny how life works. When I joined the Corps, I never dreamed I would go to a charming country like Britain and meet the shining love of my life. The fact is, before Pat and I came together, true happiness was an elusive notion, but that changed when I met Pat. I saw what joyfulness genuine, heartfelt compassion for people and her willingness to engage them. Often, strangers would gravitate towards her and spill out their life stories, seeking her understanding and comfort. Always optimistic, Pat wouldn't take many negatives to heart. Instead, she would point out the positives, impart enthusiasm and hope to anyone listening. From the outset, Pat projected a gregarious sense of humor and a joyful personality. As a staunch Scot, she loved playful banter, lively debates, standing firm on what she believed.

I watched Pat reach the boarding tunnel and approach its threshold at the Los Angeles airport. That's when she did something entirely out of character. She stopped, and turned towards me with tears streaming down her face. Fear was in her eyes—yet not a whimper. Just silence. It was a dreadful scene, forever etched in my mind. Sadness obscured the customary twinkle in her eyes and stole away her captivating smile. My heart shattered into a million pieces like a broken crystal vase. I started to run to her, but she turned and vanished inside the tunnel.

As Pat disappeared into the dark boarding tunnel my heart pounded profusely. Her eerie demeanor, her sudden burst of tears stupefied me. Combined with her unusual disappearing act, and before this sad moment, there were questions about an assortment of disturbing events. Knowing Pat's honesty, answers would probably emerge. Only she could give me answers, but she was already boarding the plane out of my reach. Time was running out and I had to act immediately. But I was numb with despair.

I couldn't shake off the dread, the severe anxiety of not knowing. Pat and I had always sensed what the other needed and I felt danger. This disturbance must've been beyond her control, something dreadful hidden deep within her thoughts. I had never seen such empty despair in her eyes. Any situation rarely overcame her; even if her troubles seemed overwhelming, she would find a way to persevere, remain optimistic, overcome with a smile. That's who she was and that's why I was baffled.

I called her cell phone, but no answer. I had to keep my composure, my sensibilities. I had to do something, anything to impede Pat's apparent breakdown. At the same time, I felt constrained, at a loss for what I could do. I had to talk to her, but my chances were dwindling. They had sealed off the tunnel ramp and were starting to rev up the jet engines.

Pat was definitely in trouble, and I had to see her again before she left. Suddenly, an urge to charge towards the ramp door came over me. I had to know she would be okay.

I darted towards the tunnel door, dodging aggressively through a sea of loitering passengers. The disruption triggered an alarm for the airline agents; soon, I saw a couple of security guards heading my way. But I kept rushing towards the ramp door. A commotion quickly arose as airline agents waved me off, commanding me to stop, but I was determined to stop the plane and get to Pat.

Nearing the gate, I desperately tried rattling off an explanation. "I have to see my wife again. There's something wrong with her!"

The agents vehemently shook their heads and urgently gestured me to stop. "No. We can't let you. The plane is backing away."

The situation quickly escalated into a calamity. Before I went farther, the two security guards forcefully grabbed me by the arms and pulled me away, shouting, "Sir, you can't go in there!"

I would not give up. A struggle ensued. I shoved the guards back and broke away, but they quickly seized me again. Finally, it dawned on me what I was doing and I was not thinking straight. The guards kept their grip tight, both wide-eyed, alert. I regained my composure and expressed a bit of remorse.

"Guys, I'm sorry. Really. I was trying to get to my wife before the plane took off. She's not in a good way. And I don't know what's wrong with her."

One guard said, "Sorry, sir, but if it's not a real emergency, it's too late."

They loosened their grip on my arms but stayed with me. I was at an impasse. I couldn't cite a specific problem, so I couldn't claim a specific medical emergency. Besides, Pat would appear reasonably normal to others. Even so, Pat's peace of mind mattered more than my safety and well-being or the need to avoid trouble. I quietly endured a deserved verbal thrashing from the guards. They warned me

that they could've arrested me for disturbing the peace—and rightfully so. I patiently explained my predicament, giving more details about Pat's disorientation. Eventually, they understood, but it was too late to do anything there and then. I tried calling her cell phone again but made no connection.

I contemplated my next move. At that moment, I noticed something on the guards' uniforms that diverted my attention: the military-like rank stripes on their shoulders sparked a flashback—my tour in the Marine Corps—and how I met Pat in the first place. The airport guards were young and fresh, much like Marine recruits. This observation led me back to my days as a recruit in San Diego and my four-year tour in the Marines.

Immersed in the past, I thought about going to London and meeting Pat. I eagerly let my mind recall those times because it was a milestone, a path to a special relationship, a destiny. I retrieved enchanting morsels of past events—our courtship in the U.K., the most treasured moments of my life. I immediately felt better, a much-needed break. Pleasant, exhilarating memories flooded back, which nourished brief contentment and a positive attitude. I was then in a state of mind to develop a plan to reunite with Pat quickly. As always, memories of Pat and our courtship worked magic.

And now, her health and safety are in danger.

# Chapter Four

## Hometown History

Memory is the yarn of consciousness —the thought fabric of life. Pulling threads gives you fodder to spin a story, a beginning, a middle, and an ending. How long are the strings, and what is the best way to re-stitch them into a story? A story is a mosaic of words, and it's a matter of piecing the puzzle of words together. So far, this story begins near the end, with events leading to a tragic conclusion—the dramatic finale of a romantic, often adventurous journey. Only the journey starts long before that. There's more to the story, so much more.

It began when I left my hometown of Port Arthur, Texas, and joined the Marines right out of high school. Why the Marines? There wasn't a lot of logic to it. My girlfriend's dad was a former Marine and his opinion influenced me. I was intent on joining the Navy and when I told him, he said, "How about the Marines? They have the best training-the elite."

And so, it was.

*"We have a saying in the Marine Corps, and that is, 'no better friend, no worse enemy than a U.S. Marine.' We always hope for the first friendship but are certainly more than ready for the second."*

—General John F. Kelly, USMC (Ret.)

In retrospect and most importantly, an assignment in the Marines led to meeting my future wife in London—Pat—an event that sparked a life-long romantic flame. After high school, I was in a funk and needed an emotional fix, a change in direction. I suppose lots of guys feel the same at that age. But my kind of remedy differed from what others may have pursued.

This book is about snapshots of a romantic life interlaced together and grievance after losing a loved one.

After graduating from Bishop Byrne high school in 1958, I wasn't ready to go to college and good jobs were scarce. Stuck in the muck, I turned in every direction but saw no promising avenues to fit my passionate but unfocused ambition to succeed in some way. The military emerged as an attractive option. I figured an outfit like the Marine Corps would instill the discipline to mature and become a man. Luckily, the Corps also helped bring Pat into my life when they sent me to London as a Marine Embassy Guard. I never imagined being stationed for prestigious duty at an embassy in a fantastic, English-speaking country thousands of miles from home. I was lucky, luckier than some Marines who were in one dull place with the same job, same bunk for four-plus years. Even as a Marine Security Guard (MSG), the healthy, safe and reliable kind, they could've sent me anywhere—to embassies in hot spots like Iran, Lebanon, Somalia, Syria and the list goes on.

I was fortunate, and I had the feeling my duty in London would be a turning point in my life. As it happened, when I applied for embassy duty, by coincidence, Pat was leaving her hometown of Corby, England, for London. She would start her career with her first job at the American Embassy. Our kinetic paths seemed paralleled, dovetailing into a meeting at the embassy. They say matches like ours are God-sent. And I believe it. Going to London was a new start in my life, much like when my dad and his family left Sicily for America. It was a new life for them.

At the age of 16, before highways and air travel in Sicily, Dad, his four brothers and one sister all trekked 100 miles from San Biagio Platani to Palermo. They boarded the ship *Algeria,* and according to the manifest, they first sailed to Naples. From Naples, they went to the U.S. with plans to meet their parents, who had immigrated earlier. Grandfather "Gaglio" had been a successful pharmacist but chose to leave an ominous life in Sicily. The Mafia, the abuse of political power, a slow economy and protection rackets were widespread.

On February 4, 1907, after deboarding *Algeria* at Ellis Island, Dad and his siblings checked in with U.S. immigration. They barely knew enough English to get through it. Grandfather Giovanni Battista and Grandmother Caterina (Neri) Gaglio had arrived earlier to lay the groundwork for family settlement. At some point at Ellis Island, authorities changed the family name from "Gaglio" to "Gallio," because they are pronounced the same in Italian.

## Background Parallels

When Pat grew up in Aberdeen, Scotland, and later in England, it was during and after the war. It was a time of recovery, as was the case in the U.S. Pat's mom talked about times spent in the bomb shelters with Pat and her sister Jackie during German bombing attacks—something we never had to deal with in America. The biggest concern was surviving the depression, which in some ways was worse for Britain than America. They, too, had to watch every penny, or as they say in British parlance, "pence." Also, the British lifestyle may have been simpler and more self-reliant than here in America. I don't believe Pat had many toys as a child, but she talked about making up games, playing sports at school and the beautiful parks. And I learned first-hand, Pat's mom habitually knitted clothing, usually bulky woolen sweaters or shawls—very much needed in the cold English and Scottish winters. She knitted me several beauties over time, and most assuredly, I needed them in the British winters and the Northeastern U.S. when we lived there later.

In the 40s and 50s in Britain, "making do and mending" was a mantra for survival, just as in America. People hardly had enough fuel to burn for heat and survive the bitterly cold weather. Understandably, there wasn't much discretionary spending in that era. Compared to America, homes in Britain were small, lacking space to store many things. Pat wore a school uniform, a common practice in the U.K. Back then, refrigeration was also scarce. Not many people could afford to leave any excess food for the next meal or keep it before it spoiled. Usually, refrigeration was a cut-out cubby-hole in the wall, surrounded by marble. The marble absorbed cold from outside and transferred it to the food. They bought perishable foods in small quantities to avoid spoilage and cooked every day. In community gardens, folks grew vegetables in a plot of land shared by neighbors.

There was great camaraderie throughout Britain. People had a sense of togetherness, helping one another. Everyone had to sacrifice, but it fostered unity and the British spirit of solidarity and endurance. As in America, Rock 'n Roll began in the early 50s, and the Brits also had "garage bands." Many stars launched careers in the trendy genre' of Rock 'n Roll and spin-off styles. Elvis and others came along with the embryonic "Rockabilly," which was a big step in the evolution of Rock. But all the while, jazz-based Rhythm & Blues remained a staple.

Pat and I appreciated the same music genres, including Country & Western, akin to Scotland's bouncy "Highland Fling" music. It was a testimony to Pat's heritage and her inborn talent and passion for dancing and singing. C&W music was a derivative of traditional European music—a blend of upbeat styles brought over by European immigrants, including Italian accordion, Scottish and Irish folk ballads, and Celtic fiddle music.

So, as it happened, Pat and I were on converging paths toward one another. After Pat's family moved to England from Scotland when she was eleven years old, some relatives remained in Scotland —three aunts and several cousins, particularly in Aberdeen. Just as in my childhood, she grew up with relatives her age with whom she was very close. Pat was always active, perky and playful. Naturally, everyone loved being with her. Pat, her sister Jackie and their parents, were a close family. I don't ever recall any severe drama in the Marshall family. It must've been traumatic for the Marshalls when Pat decided to go to London, live there and start a career. But they understood and went along. Much like Port Arthur, Corby was a one-industry town lacking in career opportunities. It made sense for Pat to go to London and lucky for me, we would meet at the American Embassy.

# Chapter Five

## The Connection

Have you ever felt connected with a person physically distant from you—so tightly bonded that you seem to know the person's thoughts and feelings spiritually? Fact is, we're psychopathic and telepathic creatures naturally connected by airwaves called "memes." Innate feelings, thoughts and love spread from person to person in a culture. For example, we share affection and support in a church, especially when in need. Motherly love is the greatest, then brotherly love and soul mate love. Think of a mother feeling the pain of her children, no matter how far away they are from each other—that kind of bond and thought transmission is possible.

The moment I boarded the plane to London, I felt a vague sense of meeting a person with whom I would form a close relationship. Of course, that person was Pat. Call it a hunch if you will, albeit a pleasant one.

The phenomenon was an ambiguous sensation, not consciously understandable, but robust vibes. In retrospect, it was strange, emotionally captivating, to think someone I didn't yet know would be *the* person, the one who would be my everything. At that time, Pat was an unknown, someone in a foreign country, living in a different environment, thousands of miles away. Then, we would come together at a later time and place, and she would become the central figure in my universe. She lived thousands of miles on the other side of the Atlantic, pursuing her own goals in life while I was progressing, unbeknownst to me, toward her. Both of us were unaware of each other's existence, but our coming together was inevitable, two converging paths heading for a fortuitous encounter. Call it fate. Many others have similar stories, but ours was truly magical. There were several parallels in each other's movements.

Ironically, while I was going to Marine Security Guard School in Washington, D.C., Pat moved from Corby, England, to London. She stayed with her friend Rose and her family in Islington, a Greater London residential district. She enrolled in a vocational school course to become a switchboard operator, or "telephonist," as the Brits called it. Following her completion of the study, the American Embassy hired her, and soon after that, we met I would often visit her during our courtship, taking the Tube (the subway) to the Islington station, then walking about ten blocks to Rose's house.

After we met up and as time passed, Pat and I moved through the stages of infatuation, courting and learning minute details about each other. I progressively became more intrigued with her. Pat was not spiteful. She was content with herself and completely unselfish toward others. We uncovered conflicts, but we discussed respective opinions, which sometimes led to heated debates. But we always found common ground, ending in sustained respect for each other's views. She would not brood or hold a grudge over a quarrel. We were, however, both strong-minded and had our share of mostly trivial arguments. And Pat had a way of defusing conflict, making light of it, offering forgiveness as the case may be. We knew to love oneself is to love others and that's okay, but not to the extreme. Nothing deterred our growing love for each other.

We underwent the modeling stage, assessing compatibility and cohesiveness, trying to fit each other to respective desires. Despite conflicts, we were able to identify each other's expectations and resolve disputes in our relationship. Pat was a strong-willed person and she imparted that element of strength in our relationship. An attitude of "never quit" was the moniker. Humor was one of Pat's great attributes. She could find humor in any given situation. In a misfortunate case, she could see a glimmer of humor and make you laugh it off. Pat was generous and gratuitous, and she never expected anything in return. In short, she had a natural desire to serve others.

She put everyone ahead of herself, willing to help wherever and however she could. She calibrated her moral compass to absolute truth in her relationships. She had the skill, the finesse of nurturing, the ability to recognize a person's needs immediately and the will to fulfill those needs where she could. Pat challenged me to help improve in whatever mission or goal I pursued. Her patience, words and actions were acts of encouragement and never a put-down, making our relationship solid. Pat was not the jealous kind, but she vehemently guarded her loved ones. And she was very humble in her own right, not overly ambitious, not seeking to relish the limelight. But she was always a shining star in every scenario.

Coming together with Pat was exciting to me, a kid coming from a small town in Texas with no experience in a foreign country and meeting my soul mate. The turning point, the journey, had started when I joined the Marines and embarked for London.

## The Omega and the Alpha

Leaving Port Arthur was the end of coming of age with all its juvenile antics and a new beginning in life. I realized I was taking a big step into the unknown, a different direction, a departure from the expected, but I needed to move on. I deliberated on *where I've been, where I'm going and who I want to be.* Sometimes making decisions is a crapshoot. But I didn't have time to second-guess my decision. After signing up, the Marine recruiter promptly scheduled me for the swearing-in at the Houston regional office.

The crowded Greyhound bus on the way to Houston cruised smoothly over the worn stretch of pavement, but inevitable road construction on I-10 would slow us down. It was a lonesome, tiresome journey. The passengers were quiet, with very little chatter, some napping to the bus's low, hypnotic hum and sway. Knowing I had cut my ties and gone far away I felt in limbo, facing another challenge while entering another life chapter. But I was fortunate to have already experienced independence, being willing to accept change. Besides a relatively unsheltered upbringing, in the last few years of high school, several of my cronies and I lived at an ambulance service where we were on duty 24/7, with some time off and going to school during the day. So, I already knew what it was like to be independent, live in a barracks and hang out with a bunch of amped-up guys. After pledging to the United States Constitution in Houston, I boarded a plane destined for boot camp at the Marine Corps Recruit Depot, San Diego, California.

After nearly three months of boot camp and infantry training, I was more than ready to go home for Christmas. It felt good to visit family and friends. After the Christmas holiday, I proceeded to my duty station: Twentynine Palms, California, roughly 50 miles ENE from Palm Springs. The Corps assigned me to the 1st Missile Battalion, working in supply & logistics. Then I was accepted for the Marine Security Guard program, which was a turning point, a prestigious milestone. I embraced the idea of going to the Security Guard School in Washington, D.C., and then going to a post in a foreign country. It was a far stretch from Port Arthur, as far I'd ever traveled before.

When we graduated MSG school, a dozen of us were placed on standby, awaiting assignment. Then an order came through for the

London embassy. Several MSGs in London were busted for selling cigarettes in the black market, and it was a rushed process to replace them. The rogue MSGs were quickly court-marshaled and sent back to America. After being fitted with civilian clothes at *Brooks Brothers*, we were on our way, departing from Dulles Airport.

## London Calling

Looking out a BOAC cockpit window, the panoramic view of the English terrain was gorgeous, post-card perfect, enchanting. As we approached the coast, emerald green pastures lined with white sandy beaches appeared—a beautiful, picturesque landscape. When embarking the night before, fellow MSGs and I had met the airline crew, and the captain had allowed a few of us inside the cockpit; of course, security wasn't as tight back then.

It was the first time I had been in the cockpit of an airliner. The vast array of instruments and blinking lights on the panel, the console, overhead, and on the bulkheads was mind-boggling. In little time, the De Havilland Comet 4 jet traversed the Atlantic and approached England; from our perspective, flying into this beautiful landscape was like gliding over a giant, multicolored carpet. We landed at Heathrow Airport, a central hub for international flights twelve miles west of London. Heathrow is the fifth-largest airport globally; in one of its busiest years, it processed 78 million passengers.

The place was a crowded zoo, with people hurrying back and forth from one place to another. Hordes of shoulder-to-shoulder people scampered through hallways, up and down escalators, in and out of boutique shops. We collected our luggage and boarded a bus headed for the American Embassy. The embassy occupied the Neo-Georgian style "McDonald House," across the street from Grosvenor Park, in the upscale area of Mayfair. The embassy was near the colossal Hyde Park and main artery Oxford Street, which offers a host of unique department stores such as Marks and Spencer, Selfridges and Harrod's.

Navigating through London, the first thing you notice is the old stone-faced Victorian and Edwardian buildings darkened with coal smoke. Builders artfully scrunched them together, forming a continuous string of row housing along a street. Despite our weariness from lack of sleep and jet lag, we were pivoting in our seats, gawking at the people and scenery, anxious to learn what experiences this new country would bring.

## History at the Doorstep

None of us Marines had traveled very far from our home cities in the United States. So, moving to England with its novel atmosphere was an exciting transition from what we had known in the States to other customs, scenes and routines. Embracing and adapting to the British lifestyle was easy, painless, enjoyable. Although we knew this was no vacation, we were eager to explore the city, the charming countryside and its rolling green hills dotted with bold, historic castles stretching skyward. The relocation opened up the vast annals of the entire breathtaking history of the United Kingdom. I had vivid images of knights jousting, wealthy young men fencing, Dukes and Lords dueling with pistols as their elegantly dressed ladies watched from a distance.

We roamed around sightseeing at every opportunity, enjoying the landscape with acute curiosity, impressed by everything, including girls in trendy clothes, stylish hair-dos and high-heel shoes. Their fashion was different, ranging from avant-garde to conservative. We found everyone in the U.K. to be amicable and easy to relate to. The truth is, most Brits generally like Americans.

Our first living quarters was quite the place: a hotel on Oxford Street, a classy area located a few blocks from the embassy; its convenient location helped us get acquainted with the immediate area. For Marines, living in such an upscale place was an unexpected pleasure, especially after living in spartan barracks back in the States. Another treat was the daily food deliveries. As if by magic, fixings for a healthy breakfast appeared outside our door: six pint-bottles of milk with cream on top and a dozen fresh eggs. Doorstep dairy delivery was an outdated practice in U.S. hotels by then, but the British people had maintained this charming tradition. Milk and eggs were our entire diet; it was sparse but enjoyable.

At that time, the restaurant food in London was somewhat dull. Most British people preferred bland cuisine versus American-style spicy recipes. These days, however, food connoisseurs regard London as host to a wide array of the best ethnic and geographic cuisines globally, but to us, dining at typical eateries was nothing to write home about. On paydays we would customarily have lunch or dinner at the upscale American Club in central London, a place modeled explicitly for American expatriates. The meals were close to American cuisine but still not identical—British versions of American food were not genuinely authentic. Before I met Pat, food was food; I paid little attention to different styles and cuisines, as long as it was nutritious.

When Pat entered my world, everything changed for me. I started looking at life differently. While courting, we'd go to the American Club and other restaurants and experiment with various foods together. Though we often went to less expensive eateries, just being together was ample for a romantic setting. And our fallback favorite was fish wrapped in newspaper and chips (French Fries) with a sprinkle of malt vinegar. Pat's all-time favorite was a chicken fried steak meal served at the American Club.

## 1 Grosvenor Square

After spending a few weeks in Oxford Street hotel, we moved into an upscale apartment building known as Boydell Court, St. John's Wood, London, NW8. I shared a two-bedroom apartment with Sergeant Jerry Cramer—a Glen Campbell look-alike—from Little Rock and Corporal Lance Slater from Houston. The apartment was a luxury. Great for private dates and other social events. We alternated individual use of the place during weekends off for an evening. And an opportunity to enjoy a Texas-style steak dinner with Pat. Unfortunately, they later transferred us to different barracks-style quarters because of a leadership change and a budget issue.

We first guarded the original American Embassy building at 1 Grosvenor Square. But soon afterward, we moved into a new, modern building across Grosvenor Square. Many Americans worked in the Grosvenor Square area, and the Brits had dubbed the section "Little America." That original embassy building had the old-styled punch clocks at strategic points, following a strict guard schedule. While making the rounds, we became intimately familiar with practically every inch of the place, which had a unique character of its own; I could sense the building's history in my bones—it had a certain mystic aura of transcendence to extraordinary events of the past. No one knew the high-powered secrets hidden in the walls; if they could speak, no doubt, they would speak volumes about fascinating incidents witnessed there over the years, critical conversations between diplomats and high-ranking officials. It was astonishing to be at a place where discussions and historical events had unfolded, of which only a few men would ever know, but the walls of the embassy had absorbed.

Rules at the London embassy were different from other posts; one of the most baffling was standing guard duty without handguns or rifles. Our .38 S&W Specials were locked up in a file cabinet. We were only allowed to carry a flashlight and a policeman's truncheon. Aside from clubs and other non-lethal weapons, the regular British street police did not carry firearms. Only select units and those assigned to Northern Ireland carried weapons. But since the outset of the Vietnam War, rules have changed because Global threats are profuse now.

The old embassy building had great sentimental value. The time-worn structure had lots of charm and history and it was my primary reference point for London. Unfortunately, they demolished the building a few years ago. It will always fondly remain in my thoughts.

A colorful reference is the opening scene of the 1960 suspense-thriller movie *Midnight Lace*—filmed on location at 1 Grosvenor Square. A gallery of personal experiences scrolls out. In the film, the main character—Doris Day—walks out of the embassy, strolls through foggy Grosvenor Square, then hears an eerie voice threatening to kill her within a month. It's a classic that also stars Rex Harrison and John Gavin. I've lived some of those same scenes and felt the chills, although my experiences were about romance and courtship. A lot was going on the day I first saw Pat coming through that same door-way. My eyes were fixed entirely on her; she looked like a glistening diamond. Little did I know I was looking at my future bride. And soon afterward, I encountered an up-close meeting with Pat for the first time.

# Chapter Six

## Courtship

My life dramatically changed when Pat and I came together. She was more than just a gorgeous face. Her beauty also emanated from within, from the soul. She had an alluring personality that captured your attention like a magnet. Like everyone else in her life, I gravitated towards her inch by inch, minute by minute. She was also entertaining and a powerful stimulus for looking at the bright side and happiness. I discovered that she was purely passionate and comforting after becoming more intimately involved with her. She would become the sole captor of my affection.

### Sighs at First Sight

When I first saw Pat, I had just gotten off routine guard duty, sitting in the hallway waiting for our morning debrief meeting with several other MSGs. When she appeared through the embassy doors, I did a double-take, then I felt a sudden charge of attraction. But I held back on saying anything to Pat that morning. We were on official duty and it wasn't the time nor the place to talk with her. But I instantly wanted to know everything about her. Like an electromagnetic pulse, I immediately gravitated towards her.

Consequently, I fought the urge. Pat had an alluring personality and a positive aura about her. All heads turned her way when she entered the building. And she certainly had all my attention.

I later found out Pat was a telephone operator working in the communications room at the embassy. Pat had to walk past six ogling Marines every morning to get to her office. Undoubtedly, she felt the gazes laid on her. Understandably, it was an embarrassing ordeal for a cute, chic eighteen-year-old. Masculine stares that examined her up and down were undoubtedly embarrassing. The roughly 30-yard hallway must have seemed a mile-long runway and Pat wasn't happy with the attention. The closer she approached the end of the hall, the faster her pace, practically sprinting her way to her office.

Every morning after guard duty, I anxiously waited for her. I believe everyone else did too. She provided a spark of brightness in a dull hallway congested with Marine testosterone. And I sensed competition was brewing amongst us.

She would enter through the bulky embassy doors into the foyer, peer down the long *hall of embarrassment* with a reluctant look on her face. Pat also had to walk in front of a group of Marines sitting on benches in the lobby, waiting for a debrief meeting. I believe she sometimes hesitated before taking the first step down the hallway.

She would bow her head down, fix her eyes on the floor and walk in a quick-time way past us with short, choppy steps. Her stiletto heels would echo around the hall, announcing her arrival with a continuous *click-click-click* against the marble floor. It resembled a fast-tempo metronome reverberating off the walls. Every morning, she clicked her way down the hall hurriedly with a coating of blush on her cheeks.

As if sending hungry gazes towards her way wasn't enough, we mimicked the sound of her stilettos with simulated marching against the floor. Regrettably, that added more torment during her trek to the telephone room. We presupposed she would take it in good stride. We cadence-stomped our feet in lock-step with her heel-clicks, and it sounded like a goose-marching army. She would tilt her head further with her face turning crimson and as a result, would quicken her pace one step at a time. Her footsteps would stop, then the sound of the telephone room doors clanging shut would loudly resonate in the hallway.

## Voice to Voice, Face to Face

Somewhere along the line, cupid's arrow plunged deep into my heart and I had to act fast. If I didn't make a move for her, I suspected one of the other Marines would surely try and I didn't want to chance not being the first. I telephoned her practically every day to arrange a date. From the outset, she always put me off. "I've got another engagement," she would say. It was a challenge, but her rejections made me even more determined to make her mine. I consistently called, possibly annoying her until she agreed to go out with me once we met face-to-face. Finally, one day after guard duty and after a quick change of clothes, I went to the PX, bought some groceries and stopped by the embassy. Call it fate; we crossed paths outside the embassy by chance. As I was going in, she was coming out. We met in the vestibule doorway and faced each other eye-to-eye in a small enclosure. Up close, she was stunningly beautiful, and I was a mess—unshaven, carrying a lumpy bag of groceries.

For the first time, we were face-to-face. While caught between me and two sets of doors, Pat looked like a cute rabbit in a trap. And I didn't mind being trapped with her.

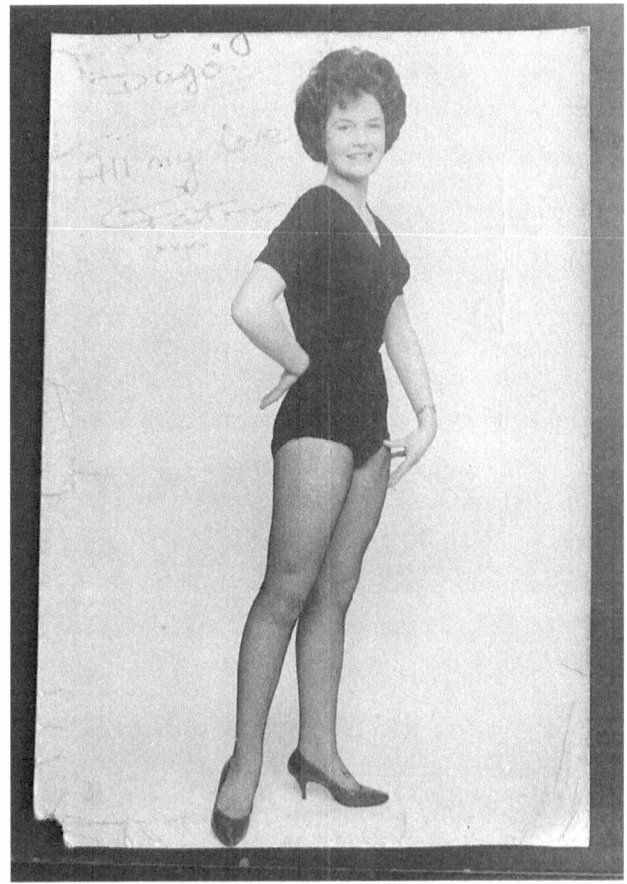

*Pat at ballet classes, London 1959*

"Hey, . . . it's me, Lou," I said rather awkwardly. I just wanted to start talking with her outside the telephone calls, but her response caught me off-guard. Instead of greeting me back with a smile, she only leveled a flat look on her face.

"And so?" She said with a rather cavalier attitude. Then she cocked her head and looked at me quizzically.

So, where do I go from here? My thoughts were scattered. After a sleepless night of guard duty, I was very uncool that auspicious day. I hadn't shaved and was in drab civilian clothes. That certainly was not the first impression I wanted to make on the girl who fascinated me. My tenacity strengthened and determination moved up a notch. I tried to focus on the challenge at hand. I may not have looked my best, but I figured she must have seen me in my dress blues.

I said, "How about getting together for dinner?"

"Sorry, can't talk now; I need to go. Call me later." She turned and walked away.

The put-off made me more determined. Convincing Pat to agree on a date with me was a worthwhile pursuit. She used a variety of "I have an engagement" excuses for several weeks. I thought she was putting me off because we worked in the same place and wanted to avoid distasteful gossip." As it turns out, Pat did have a busy schedule. She sang in a band, and on weekends they booked her at upscale pubs in London. Pat had a clear, crisp voice like Doris Day when singing pop and soft Sarah Vaughn elegance when she sang the blues.

Pat was also a ballet-trained dancer and an accomplished athlete. The more I learned about her, the more intriguing she was. Pat had a happy, playful presence that voided negatives. But she could also be stubborn, adamant about her beliefs and principles. Once she made up her mind about something, the Scottish bravado, the feistiness set in. Debating with people seemed like a sport to her. She made it amusing, entertaining, especially when she would inevitably win. She could outwit anyone.

She teased her luxurious hair, which was the fashion in those days. The style added a tad more height to her stature. When Pat spoke, she radiated positive energy, along with an atmosphere of joy. Her cheerful personality accented her internal and external beauty. Being with her felt delightful to the point where you didn't want to leave her. Her personality traits included intuitive awareness, innate passion and empathy for people.

We often shared a boxed lunch in the quiet and well-kept garden in Grosvenor Square Park. President Franklin Roosevelt's statue overlooked our favorite park bench. It stood there above our heads with the metal exterior gleaming under the sunshine. Roosevelt's wife, Eleanor, unveiled the memorial in 1948, fronted by the American Embassy. The statue is a significant landmark in London that emphasizes American relations with the British. John Adams first established an American mission there in 1875. The Park had been the traditional home to the official American presence in London since then.

*Embassy Marine Guard Detachment – London, 1960*

The Park in Grosvenor Square comprises an array of beautiful and aromatic plants and flowers, an exotic retreat in the middle of a teeming city. The garden emanated many different colors when it was sunny. Holly hedge along its perimeter, the park is astonishingly peaceful, filled with a mosaic of color and chirping birds. Somehow, nature's birds eclipsed the traffic noise from Oxford Street a few blocks away. The Park was a special place where Pat and I enjoyed intimate times together.

Our favorite bench was at the center of the expanse of green, manicured grass, and flowers surrounded us and provided us with the much-needed romantic setting. I had not realized how deprived I had been of love until I met Pat. She always lit up my mood, even on dreary days. The garden was also a perfect place for a romantic stroll. We would walk around and talk for hours. The Park was ideal for us, lost in affection and conversation, merely existing together. Our world was there and then. Outside of that, the world seemed irrelevant. No work-related issues, no strict protocols, no protests, none of it was on my mind.

Pat and I steadily dated during my two-year tour in London. On my weekends off each month, we spent time with Pat's family in Corby, in central England. We would leave after I finished the rigorous Friday schedule of all-night, round-robin guard duty, 8-hours on, 8-hours off before the weekend.

On Saturday mornings after duty, Pat and I would rush to catch a train at St. Pancras Station in central London. The train, dubbed "Beetle Bomb," was an old steam engine type only capable of reaching speeds far less than the modern, 100 mile-per-hour trains of today. After downing a bag of Licorice "All Sorts" candy, which became an addiction, I would regularly fall asleep minutes after rolling out of St. Pancras. Much to the chagrin of other passengers, I would snore most of the way to Corby, causing raised eyebrows and frowns. Pat avoided the glaring glances by reading a book. She buried her nose in a book and would not face them. My short, crew-cut hair and a Texas drawl confirmed I was a "Yank," which probably added to her embarrassment. Fortunately, there are more Yank likes than dislikes.

I convinced Pat to meet me for lunch. And I worked hard to make a better impression. I tried being charming and mature. Maybe I stretched it too much at the risk of exaggeration. After all, she was only 18 years old, living in London with a friend and family. Her hometown of Corby—an industrial center—was some 100 miles north of London. She was a naïve girl despite being so cautious, so resistant. After going on a quest to win her over, I finally met her family. They were a close-knit, humorous bunch who loved to socialize.

## Life in an English Town

I'll never forget meeting Pat's mother. It was in my apartment, just before going to dinner. She looked at me, turned to Pat and said, "Is this the best you can do?"

Pat smiled. "I guess."

I said, "Well, I'm not that bad!"

They laughed. I joined in laughter. That evening, I took Pat and her mom for dinner. And we had a delightful time with more laughter.

Pat and I were with her relatives at the Highland Games in Corby on one occasion. The Highland Games—a Celtic celebration—are held in Spring and summer throughout Britain and other countries. The games are central to an open market, competition in Scottish piping, drumming, dancing and athletic events. Pat's dad Albert used to run track in the Games and he was good at it. Pat must've inherited his speed and endurance.

Unfortunately, I discovered an element who didn't like Americans at the Games. Pat's cousin and his fiancé, Pat, and I were in a tented market area near the vegetable stands. A few teenagers gathered several stalls away and stood next to the coconut stand. One of them picked up a coconut and wound up to hurl the hairy fruit at me. Pat's cousin, an off-duty policeman, spotted the culprit and ran towards him. I was looking the other way and had no idea what was happening. It was a stroke of luck that Pat's cousin knew the hurler and stopped him. Otherwise, it would've gotten ugly.

## British Ways

Before long, weekends in Corby with Pat's family became a tradition. And I thoroughly enjoyed it on off-duty weekends. Although Pat and I would occasionally enjoy a steak dinner back in my apartment, being surrounded by her family was a pleasure. On Saturdays, when in Corby, we would go to the open markets. It would consist of a lineup of vendor booths displaying goods in the middle of the town square. The various specialty shops such as meat markets, produce and dry goods would be along the perimeter. You could buy practically anything in the open market.

While shopping, we would pause for brunch at a restaurant. Brunch in the U.K. was a big treat. I usually had eggs and a mix of British-style grilled meats, including black pudding and toast. I would wash it down with a cup of milky, caramel-colored tea. You learn to like British tea; it has a unique flavor. Once you get used to it, like coffee, it's habit-forming.

After shopping, it was back to the bungalow for a day of lounging and watching sports on the TV and snacking. Pat, her mom and sister Jacqueline also had their Saturday routine, sometimes visiting family and friends. Pat's aunt Rita would regularly come over to play cards in the evening.

Compared to a treadmill pace in America, the laid-back regimen of a small village in the U.K. was to cherish and I recall uniquely good times. We had several experiences that, to this day, prompt peace, relaxation and fellowship.

On Sundays, we would walk to the village pub. There would be no traffic on the streets on our way there. My routine was to have a sandwich, a pint or two of draught beer and a game of darts. I honed my skills at playing darts and mingling with the pub crowd as the token "Yank." The weekend schedule was a way of life, especially in small villages. Going to the markets and socializing at pubs, where there were not only dart games but snooker, pool, skittles and sometimes a small band.

On the matter of sandwiches, here's a tip: if you want a ham and cheese sandwich, be sure to tell the bartender, "Ham and cheese in the same sandwich." Otherwise, you may get a surprise. My Marine buddy Jerry and I learned that lesson when we first arrived in London. We each ordered a ham and cheese sandwich at a pub. The bartender served two sandwiches each, a ham sandwich and a cheese sandwich.

Back at the cottage, and after a short nap, we had Sunday dinner. After dinner, we went back to the pub, played some darts, gathered around a table and sipped after-dinner drinks. I fell deeply in love with the girl and the British culture. A piece of my heart will always be its capture.

# Chapter Seven

## London Town

"All is good; treat each day, each minute as a 'present' from God," Pat would say. She always looked at the sunny side of life.

Her words rung true. With her at my side, everything in London was more buoyant, more intriguing, more gratifying. Pat always added cheer, optimism, positivity to her presence. Her attitude was that even the least likeable aspects of London—the pungent fumes from smoldering charcoal in fireplaces, the diesel emissions from cabs and cars—were part of the city's unique ambiance. Pat's pleasant demeanor eclipsed even that of most Londoners, a jolly lot as a rule. Even during the so-called Cold War, London's atmosphere was carefree, friendly, refreshing, stimulating. The people were generally courteous, living to enjoy life and each other. The *joie de vivre* was terrific, yet not surprising, considering their struggle to survive the depression and World War II. Through it all, the British people have retained their cheerful tenacity despite all the trials and struggles life has thrown at them.

That cheerful tenacity is apparent even on a busy street. Double-decker buses were iconic. Black "Hackney" cabs had plenty of head-room originally built for top hats. And slick maneuvering motorbikes weaving through traffic are daily requisites of the London environment. You learn to move with London's fast-paced tempo to the harmony of buses and cabs buzzing about and teeming crowds of people roaming the sidewalks, slipping in and out of shops. Like other cities, I suppose, but with its unique music of the streets, it's sounds. Then there are the old, elegant buildings and beautiful flower gardens that bring out London's unique beauty and contribute to its distinctive lifestyle as in small villages. Consider the neighborhood pubs, where locals gather for a lager, a sandwich, a game of darts and fellowship.

Getting around London was easy. You could travel by cab, bus, or train—your choice. That's another thing I liked about Britain. With public transportation, you don't need a car. The distinctive leathery scent of an Austin London Black Cab was unforgettable; the distinct smell stays with you for hours. The rattle of diesel engines added vigor to the city's character and blended with London's lively atmosphere. Double-decker buses, also used for touring, were a great way to get around and sight-see. As with these iconic coaches, you had to learn the routes when riding the Tube. You need to know which bus line to choose, but there are color-coded maps to help navigate your way. When you got off, you were likely within walking distance of your destination. If not, there would be a taxi stand nearby.

## Happy Adventures

Besides going to the jazz clubs in Soho, the movies and restaurants, Pat and I often went to fairs where we played typical games and endured thrilling rides. One day early in our relationship, in a booth at a local carnival, I tossed balls at bowling pins to impress Pat.

Getting her to date me had been a big ordeal. I never took her "Yes" as a carte blanche arrangement. After several tries at the booth, I won a prize: a stuffed toy bird nearly as large as Pat. The furry flyer had a 9-inch beak with long, dangling arms and legs, large golf ball eyes, a fuzzy cap and a ridiculous facial expression; it was a bit like Sesame Street's Big Bird, but this was ten years before they introduced that yellow icon to the world's culture in 1969. Pat looked ecstatic as she held the bird close to her chest like a child with their favorite toy. It felt good knowing I helped put a smile on her face. Afterward, Pat and I boarded a double-decker bus and the big critter sat on Pat's lap back home. The other passengers had mixed reactions—some eyed the toy with beaming smiles, others showed their distaste with muffled remarks. She paid no attention to them as she admired her new friend. Pat grinned as she fiddled with the bird's gangly arms and stroked his soft fur. She was delighted with the prize. The beige-colored bird stayed at Pat's lodging for a long while. Stretched out, it was nearly as tall as Pat and its facial expression with bulging eyeballs seem to stare at you with a mocking, silly grin. The goofy image was entertaining. It made you laugh. It appeared to be a cross between a penguin and an albatross, but not explicitly. Pat named the giant rag doll "Louie-Lou," to which I said, "I know I have a beak, but it's not *that* long!"

Pat was always upbeat and entertaining. Spending a lot of time together made us realize we were truly compatible. Sure, Pat and I were not perfect, we had our occasional spats, but they only lasted a few minutes. We were both headstrong, so we usually called a truce, made-up. Nothing was worth arguing over and Pat had a way of introducing humor, cutting it short. She had a way of neutralizing stubbornness, make me smile and forget about it. These small battles turned out to be silly and humorous. Pat's positive vibes dominated and the conflict diminished.

What's more, Pat was the type of person who was often delighted over small things. She would find happiness in every little thing—

something I had once deemed unimportant. I still remember the first time I saw her unrestrained exuberance. It was late autumn, the season for chestnuts in London. Pat and I strolled down Oxford Street on one zesty evening, across from the famous Selfridges department store, catty-corner from Keysign House, where I stood guard duty and where Pat would sneak me pork pies for lunch.

Pat hesitated and said, "Ahh, I smell something. Roasted chestnuts. Let's get some!"

I got a big whiff. "Great idea!"

My taste buds instantly awakened. The unique fragrance of chestnuts—most likely imported from Italy and roasting on a coal-fired cooker—was irresistible; the warm, delicious scent wafted through the foggy air straight to our nostrils and guided us towards a street vendor. We approached the guy tending to a cart brazier, a portable heater fueled by coal. Shrouded in a heavy coat with a thick plaid scarf around his neck and a woolen beret cap, the man eagerly greeted us in the heavy Cockney accent common among London street vendors.

"How many, Luv?" he asked Pat with a smile.

"Two bags, please."

The vendor nodded and handed two bags to Pat with charcoal-tarnished fingers poking through fingerless gloves.

"Ta," Pat replied—British jargon for "thanks."

We paid the man and continued on our way while savoring warm, delectable chestnuts. The totality of it is a simple yet extraordinary experience native to London.

One day at a carnival, a Ferris wheel mishap caused Pat to inadvertently open to me more than she had before. We were enjoying the ride until it suddenly lurched to a stop and set the gondolas to rocking back and forth, raising a frighteningly harsh metallic din. Pat grabbed my arm and squeezed tight.

"Lou, I'm scared!"

"Don't worry, Sweetie. Just hang on."

Our gondola continued swaying precariously about 60 feet above the ground. People in other gondolas voiced their alarm. The Ferris Wheel started again with a sudden jerk, followed by another hard stop. We heard screams around the giant wheel.

"Yikes!" I muttered. The ordeal was beginning to scare me too.

Pat white-knuckled the side of the gondola with one hand and clenched me with the other. She snuggled closer and we felt as one.

## The View from Way Up There

I supposed Pat had developed a stronger fear for Ferris Wheels after the incident. But that didn't stop her, years later, from riding the London Eye, the world's tallest Ferris wheel at the time it was built— 442.9 feet high and 393.7 feet in diameter— spinning over 3.75 million riders each year around its orbit. With large, oval-shaped pods that can hold 25 people each, the Eye can carry 800 passengers on one go-round. The day we rode the Eye was a clear day with few clouds and you could see miles in the distance. Pat wasn't insecure as before, partly because she was too busy joking with everyone and playing a tour guide role. Though we were very high in the sky, she was relaxed and cheery.

She pointed at a distant structure and said, "Windsor Castle!"

Everyone keenly eyed the Royal Palace, its grandeur and the Queen's majestic second home. Although located about 20 miles west of our location, the castle's three-walled areas were visible. And the castle roof reaching into the clear blue sky was a remarkable sight.

Pat and I had toured Windsor Castle one brisk, windy day while on a double-date with my fellow MSG Jerry and his future wife Diane, a Foreign Service Officer. Windsor is near the River Thames, a few miles upstream from London. Known as Britain's architectural heritage and the Queen's preferred home, it's the oldest, largest occupied castle in the world. I still have a photo of Pat and me on that delightful day at Windsor. Pat was cute, chic, and as always, displayed her magical, infectious smile. An instant before Jerry snapped the photo, a gust of wind flared the pleated skirt and puffy petticoats Pat wore that day. The dress reached from her waist to inches below her knees. Embarrassed about the situation, Pat noted on the back of the photo, "My skirt was not that short; it was a windy day."

One of our favorite places was Rockingham Castle, located two miles outside Corby. Pat and I visited this quaint castle frequently and of note, I sat at the desk where the famous Scottish poet and lyricist Robert Burns had penned some of his works. Burns used to visit the castle during his travels. Historically, the charming fortress was a royal bastion and hunting lodge high on a hill in Rockingham Forest. Climb the stairs, look through the gun turrets, and witness a lush green carpet of grass leading to the small village with thatch rooftops. Near the town, modest headstones dot a small cemetery. It's a post-card-perfect scene. The castle has a rich 900-year history, and Pat and I felt the spiritual vibes and savored the ethos. Near Pat's home, we often visited Rockingham and it has a special place in memory.

Pat and I would also attend embassy functions and staff parties back in London. She was a big hit with the State Department Security Director, the officer in charge of our unit. In another photo, Pat and the officer are standing together with joyful grins. And we had community-based events sponsored by our MSG unit.

*Pat and Lou with Security Officer at Embassy Event –*
*London, 1960*

One year, the MSGs organized a Christmas party for disabled children—an active participation philanthropic effort. We held the event
in the embassy cafeteria, the same place where President John F.
Kennedy would address the embassy staff in June 1961. Pat and I
chaperoned five-year-old twins, a boy and a girl, both quadriplegic
and unable to do much of anything. That day, we were their
guardians and we stayed with them throughout the event. This party
was the children's first time attending a public affair without their
parents or caregivers. And we had a taste of caring for children.
When the twins' parents invited us over for dinner to show their
appreciation, we gratefully accepted.

## A Window on History

In May 1960, several London Marines, including myself, were sent
to Paris to augment a U.S. military detachment assigned to the
upcoming summit in Paris, an event arranged to ease tensions
between the Western nations and the USSR. President Eisenhower,
Prime Minister Macmillan of the U.K., President de Gaulle of

France, and Chairman Khrushchev of Russia met in Paris's Elysée Palace. We stood guard there for a meeting of the most influential leaders globally at the time—a significant historical event that became ignominiously famous in an unexpected way.

At the height of the Cold War, tensions between the Western powers and the USSR were severe. The U.S. and other Western countries were conducting an aggressive political campaign against communism in general and the USSR. Following World War II, the expansion of Soviet power had brought economic suppression to much of eastern Europe and a shake-up of the geopolitical world. Both sides were conducting covert operations and espionage, and the Soviets tried hard to prevent their citizens from fleeing to the West. The Berlin Wall had been built down the middle of a city brutally divided between communist oppression and Western liberty. Armies patrolled both sides, and it was a tangible symbol of the tensions of the Cold War. The Paris summit intended to arrange a compromise in the Berlin situation.

Two weeks before the summit was to take place, a serious international incident occurred. Russia shot down an American spy plane known as the U2. The Russians captured the pilot, Francis Gary Powers, and charged him with espionage. he U2 incident shot down the summit as well: an infuriated Khrushchev demanded an apology from Eisenhower for breaching mutual trust and spying on his country in a highly emotional confrontation. Eisenhower refused to apologize.

Khrushchev raised his hands over his head and said, "As God is my witness, my hands are clean and my soul is pure."

Who could believe him? The leader of a regime that had imprisoned and murdered millions of its people? The meeting ended soon afterward; rather than ease tensions, it increased them and the Cold War raged on. Our stay in Paris was cut short and they shuttled us back to London. But the Paris experience was fascinating. It stands out in my mind for its historical nature and a different reason—a culinary one. The Marine House in Paris was near a coffee factory and the aroma of freshly ground coffee beans permeated the air at all hours. It was a steady caffeine lift that many Marines most appreciated after guard duty. It also reminded me of the delicious aroma that still tinged the air in Beaumont—and does to this day—from the Seaport Coffee Company plant there. Since that time, the smell of coffee reminds me of Paris, a vibrant city Pat and I would eventually visit on vacations.

## The Ghosts of London

London has many "haunted" sites and some say the U.S. Embassy satellite office on Brook Street was one of them. Unlike Keysign House bordering Oxford Street, the isolated Brook Street building was dark and creepy; and there were rumors of a haunting. Embassy staff only occupied the top three floors. An accordion-style security gate in the stairway blocked access from other floors after all had left the building. I ensured the gate was secure and continued inspection. Suddenly, I heard the chain on the gate rattle. Then I heard the gate slam shut. I raced down the stairs to the gated portal. Nothing had changed—it was shut tight and locked. I rushed to the back door. It was wide open. I went outside, but no one was in sight. Traffic whizzed by and a devil's breath swirled down the dark back-door tunnel abyss. I locked the door, paused, and thought over the events. Nothing made sense.

Aside from the Brooke Street office, Pat and I visited the dimly lighted Madame Tussaud's Wax Museum, which is the ultimate in spookiness. We seemed to be the only patrons there. The museum marketed the thrill of London's more dark and bloodcurdling aspects. The wax figures are life-size and often scary, even the normal ones not associated with the dark side. While walking past Elvis's lifelike mannequin, you would subconsciously expect him to break out in his herky-jerky hip movements singing Hound Dog. The resemblance to the natural person is uncanny.

The dungeon-like Chamber of Horrors imprints one's memory with gruesome wax creatures locked in prison cells with a display of weird crime scenes. It sends chills up and down your spine. Most riveting, the opened cells implied ghouls were roaming the dark halls. Pat and I held hands tightly as we walked past the cell-like partitions. We invariably looked over our shoulders, wasting little time scurrying out of there.

# Chapter Eight

## Journeys, Traditions and Adieus

P at and I often met at quaint restaurants and espresso bars in London on casual dates. The cozy coffee houses were widespread in Europe long before the U.S. Besides tooling around London and managing a little vacation time, we went on day trips to places like Holland and Paris. It's easy to travel within the U.K. and Europe. Cities are short hops, like going to another state in the U.S. and there are multiple travel modes. Although, the most memorable trips were going to Scotland to visit Pat's relatives in Aberdeen, a major city situated on the North Sea shores. The scenery in Scotland is breathtaking, a fantastic, picturesque wonderland.

Traveling with Pat and her mom was entertaining, albeit mainly for the two of them. When together, they always had fun. One summer, on the way to Aberdeen, I endured most of their jokes. They had elected to make fun of me the entire trip! Pat's dad, Albert, warned me about their playful antics when together. It was an awakening experience. I learned how flippant Pat and her mom could be. It was a loving, respectful relationship.

*Picnic in the Highlands – near Aberdeen, Scotland, 1961*

It wasn't the only time they poked fun at me. It started from the get-go when I first met Pat's mom in my apartment in London. I didn't realize it would be an ongoing thing. For this trip to Scotland, we rented a Mini Cooper, a small SUV designed for economy and navigating narrow, windy roads in Europe. My six-foot frame was almost longer than the car. We barely had enough room for three people.

When we took nap breaks along the way, the car was so narrow I had to lie on the back seat and hang my legs out the window. Good thing it didn't rain. Pat and her mom thought it was hilarious as they howled with laughter when I laid down, staring at the roof with my legs dangling outside. They ignored my grumbling as I tried to find a better angle to rest. When I complained, they would only chuckle more. I hardly got any shuteye because of their constant antics, their giggling. Nonetheless, I enjoyed the trip.

Once in Aberdeen, we stayed with Pat's aunt Beth and Uncle Jimmy. I met all the family, including younger cousins. Pat's cousins enjoyed learning how to play American football. It was an entirely new game, a unique experience for them. The kids lined up on two sides in the front yard and I played quarterback. We emulated impromptu pass plays. They ran out and I threw passes. We had a great time—relatives from the Carr, Urquhart, Young and McDonald families. The exposure to American-styled football was especially relevant for one family that later migrated to Canada, where there's American-style football.

We stayed with Pat's aunt Beth and uncle Jimmy. Jimmy was a piano tuner and my occasional fishing partner. One of his clients was a wealthy doctor who had a home on property bordering the River Dee, an 87-mile river that spans Wales, England and Scotland to the North Sea. In Scotland, the river swells in the mountain range of the Cairngorms in the eastern Highlands of Scotland—and runs through the Aberdeen region to the North Sea. Queen Victoria built Balmoral Castle along the river, which serves as one of the British Royal Family's regular residences. The castle is in Royal Deeside, near the village of Crathie, about 50 miles from Aberdeen—a very picturesque setting.

Freshwater seafood is abundant in River Dee, notably large Atlantic salmon, born in freshwater, migrated to the sea and then returned to freshwater to spawn. It was entertaining for Pat & me to stand on Aberdeen's "Brig o Dee" spanned over the river, watching the salmon struggle to hurdle a waterfall and travel upstream to their spawning grounds. The challenge is a contest of sheer tenacity and luck. Once over the hump and in calmer waters, their conquest was not over. The journey could take as many as six months to complete.

Jimmy had permission to fish on a stretch of the river paralleling the doctor's estate. On our fishing expedition early one morning, we were equipped with ample fly-fishing gear and a six-pack of *Newcastle Brown Ale* as we cast our lines in the rushing River Dee. We trudged along the river and caught a sizeable mess of trout and perch. Not being an avid fisherman, I learned a few tricks from Jimmy that day and was lucky to have snagged a modest number of fish. After finishing off the six-pack of ale and amassing a sizeable catch of fish, we went back to the house and dined on fried fish for brunch. Pat and her aunt Beth whipped up fish and chips, a side of blood pudding and beans. It made for a filling, delicious meal. I could quickly adopt a daily fishing-brunch routine, but I would need to live near a fresh-water stream which is hard to find in Southeast Texas. Otherwise, it wouldn't be the same.

Mingling with Pat's family always brought great enjoyment. We had picnics in the Highlands and went to pubs together. The camaraderie and humor of the Scots were forever virulent. You couldn't help but join in and have fun, whether at a gathering or touring the Scottish Highlands' gorgeous landscape.

The Highlands is also known as the place of the *Gaels* and is a fantastic place to visit. It's situated closer to heaven at its highest peak of 4,409 feet. When we were there, it was indeed a unique, exhilarating experience. After reaching its highest point, we were literally in the clouds. The scenery was postcard-perfect, accented by a cluster of puffy, snow-white clouds overhead and a band of heather amid an emerald green mountainside.

One chilly spring day, we were driving through the Highlands. We briefly stopped the car to allow a shepherd and his sheep to stroll across a dirt road. I panned the area, pegged it as a great photo-op and took advantage of it. Envision a vibrant oil painting—tones of lilac and deep purple heather against a green backdrop brushed across a mountainside. Add a cobalt blue sky, clean, fresh air, layers of puffy balls of clouds and a mist hovering close above. *Is heaven like this?* The landscape was surreal, captivating, fascinating.

Pat sat amongst the heather with her legs crooked up and arms locked around her knees. A gentle breeze brushed across her stylishly coiffed, silky auburn hair. Her hazel eyes emanated love, humor, sensuality and sincerity. A beaming smile on her creamy white, gently square face and a lovely duchess nose created the perfect portrait for a photoshoot.

She angled her head with a twinkle in her eyes and said in a classy Aberdonian accent, "How's this?"

"Perfect." I snapped a picture. Pat was like a dazzling, bright flower among various shades of purple heather. Heather's genus name "Calluna" stems from the Greek word "*kalluno*," which roughly translates "*to adorn*." That's the essence of the photo—another romantic jewel.

England and Scotland were perfect for courting the girl I loved. The rolling hills, the quaint villages, the changing seasons, the fantastic cliffs, bold castles and medieval history. Particularly in Scotland, where the people were friendly and lively, the Highlands, the beautiful fields of heather, the historical stories are unmatched. Scotland also has many interesting customs with a central theme of merriment. The Scots are happy, hearty people who cling to New Year celebrations. Scotland is the birthplace of the song "Auld Lang Syne" and the Scottish festivity for the New Year "Hogmanay." When I was preparing to leave Aberdeen and saying goodbyes to Pat's family, I had flashbacks of my first New Year's holiday in Corby, where Pat's parents lived. The family initiated me with a tradition called *First Footing*. Neighbors would visit each other and impart good wishes shortly after midnight on New Year's Eve. According to legend, First Foots—a man—would bring a shortbread gift for the table or a lump of coal for the fire. It also brought luck to have a tall, dark, handsome man to be the first to enter the house after ringing in the New Year.

Back in London, we continued to frequent jazz clubs such as Ronnie Scott's. Besides jazz clubs, we often attended other live shows together when top entertainers were in town. Once, we went to a special event at the London Palladium, where the *Dave Brubeck Quartet* was in concert. The Palladium is a famous 2,286-seat theater in the West End. The drummer, Joe Morello, was one of my favorites for jazz. Back in Port Arthur, I spent hours in Port Arthur trying to play Morello solos on my back porch using a cheap drum kit. I thought it sounded okay, but it was fake awkward sounds, not like Morello's sound at all. I didn't know what I was doing. My strokes were nothing like his smooth, accurate hits.

That night at the Palladium, when Morello played his solo in "Take Five," the audience was so quiet you could hear a pin drop. Coincidentally, my drumming instructor, Max, was also present in the audience. He had a studio in his crowded Chelsea bungalow, where he conducted weekly lessons. A few days later, I went in for my next drumming lesson. Max placed a sheet of drum music on my music stand. I gazed at a series of symbolic dots, drum notations: quarter notes, half notes, sixteenth notes, cymbal notations and a mish-mash of other drum music symbols.

He pointed to the sheet music and said, "Play this."

"What is it?"

"Morello's solo." He casually replied as if it was no big deal.

To me, it was. Max, a true professional, had transcribed Morello's entire solo in real-time while sitting in the audience, a tremendous feat. Max was an excellent instructor. By coincidence, he also taught Ringo Starr when the Beatles were ramping up their rise to stardom.

Another memorable event in 1960 was when Pat and I saw my friend Johnny Preston in London. He was on tour with Conway Twitty (*It's Only Make Believe*) and Freddy Cannon (*Way Down Yonder In New Orleans*). The British loved American entertainers. Fans packed the place and as expected, the show was incredible. Later, we visited Johnny in his hotel room, which was impressive to Pat. As a singer herself, meeting Johnny was something to behold.

*Pat in the Heather – In the Highlands near Aberdeen,*
*Scotland, 1961*

## British Traditions

Back in Corby, during my first Christmas season at Pat's house, the snow was over a foot deep. The compounded ice crystals stacked a few feet high. As heavy snowflakes floated down, they immediately stuck to the ground, forming a puffy white blanket. Little did I know they would ask me to play an essential role in their traditional holiday scene. The family chose me as the First Foot. While standing at the door in the snow with the frosty wind swirling around me, I felt weird standing in this freezing weather with coal in my hand. Since then, I was the First Foot guy when I was there. I accepted the tradition took pride in being a part of Pat's family, including the cuisine that came with it.

It took some time, but I learned to like their so-called sausage, Black Pudding, Haggis and a spiced delight called Minced Pie, a fruit-based delight customarily served at Christmas time. On the sweet side, no matter the season, Pat's special treat was Cadbury's *Flake*—chocolate flakes folded into a bar—stuck in a cone, perhaps a 99 cone of Italian gelato. It turns out, one choice food of mine was *Black Pudding,* a sort of delicacy like *Boudin*—a sausage made of combined ingredients stuffed in a casing. It's popular with and originated by Cajuns in Louisiana and Southeast Texas.

I was beginning to dread the inevitable as time went on. My tour in England was ending soon and I was running out of time. I had to leave London early and head to my next duty station: First Tank Battalion, Camp Las Pulgas, Pendleton, California.

No matter where I was, my heart was with Pat. Despite my unwillingness, the time to leave had arrived. I would miss Pat and everything about London. I couldn't say I liked leaving and going back to the States. Pat had captured my heart and I dreaded a separation. Besides our romance, she had become my best friend, a generous person, someone I could confide in and get practical advice.

It was time to bid farewell, a dull, abysmal moment. When we parted, the imagery of Pat seared my memory. Akin to a Norman Rockwell painting, snowflakes fell like graffiti from heaven against a dark gray sky. After we said our goodbyes on the platform of a stone-faced train station, Pat stood teary-eyed in a layer of foot-deep snow. I was tight with emotion, holding back emotions to avoid exacerbating Pat's sadness. I boarded the train and went to the gangway connection, where I slid a Plexiglas window down and poked my head out to see Pat. She stood motionless, patiently watching the train steam-up, nudge sluggishly away from the platform and head towards London. I leaned further out the window and waved. She forced a smile and waved back. We both struggled to keep our composure. Although, deep in our hearts, we both knew we would be together again.

Nonetheless, leaving Pat was leaving my heart behind. We dated for two years, became best friends and had an exciting, fun courtship. We fell profoundly in love over these two years. Spending a day where we wouldn't be able to see each other was unimaginable. We had become one, a significant part of each other's being.

Pat's spirit remained with me as I left her standing on the train platform. I leaned further out the train window as it gained speed. The rush of sticky wet snow and cold air crusted my hair with a silky residue, but I didn't care. I had one goal in my mind: to permanently impress her persona in memory. I fixed my gaze on Pat until she dwindled into a veil of falling snowflakes in the darkness.

On the plane going back to the States, I thought long and hard about our relationship. The further I went away from Britain, the heavier my heart. We had been together for two years. Now we would be apart by thousands of miles. She could no longer cling to me, show her smiles, shower me with attention.

Thinking about our relationship was giving me heartaches. So, I decided to focus on doing things logically, step-at-a-time. Go back to the States, settle in first and see how it goes. No matter how I diverted my thoughts, nothing could be better than my days with Pat. The farther away from her, the deeper I was falling into a black hole. And my heart was becoming progressively empty. I longed for the joy of being with her and hearing her cheery voice. I missed looking into her sparkling eyes, inspired by a cute, buoyant demeanor. I pined over everything about her deeply. By the end of each day, I felt as lonely as ever. I regarded her as a blossoming rose—a unique species of rose. This kind of love only happens once in a lifetime, burning deep in the heart.

The love I held for her ran through my veins like a raging river. I hoped that she, too, felt the same about me.

# Chapter Nine

## Proposal

Engraved in memory is the scene of Pat on the train platform in Corby, standing in a deep bed of snow waving goodbye. Nothing could divert my mind from dwelling on this image; I could hardly sleep on the plane back to the U.S. I was restless the entire flight, missing Pat, wanting her. Her face, that scene, continually scrolled across my mind and still does to this day.

I went on Christmas leave from Britain, straight home to Port Arthur, but it wasn't quite the happy occasion it should have been. Only one person could help make life more comfortable and an ocean of miles separated us. I missed Pat—all of her, everything about her. The minute I stepped foot on the airplane in London, my heart began splintering away, piece by piece.

Wherever I was, whatever I was doing, she entered my mind. I missed the loving gaze in her eyes and the atmosphere that glowed all around her.

## Absence Makes the Heart Grow Fonder

I've never been keen on long-distance relationships, yet there I was, pining over Pat from far away. I thought maybe my feelings would mellow after leaving London, making new friends, doing different things. The old saying is true: absence makes the heart grow fonder. Strangely though, the distance made me feel closer to her; we were physically apart, yet it felt more than ever like we two were as one; our hearts were one. I knew we would be together again; it was inevitable. Being away from her made me realize how much I relied on her and loved her. Pat was everywhere in my psyche. When I heard laughter, I thought of Pat. When the sun shone down, warming me, I felt her presence and sensed her soothing voice. I continually reminisced about the momentous times we'd had— times when we walked side-by-side along the streets of London doing simple things together. I needed her, longed to be in her presence, within her aura and hear her cheery voice again.

In some cases, maintaining a loving relationship can be tricky when a couple is far apart. There are temptations—love can dissipate the more you spend time away from each other—but not in our case. Pat and I shared a unique, strong sense of love that developed over two years. It's fascinating how couples are tied to each other in a relation-ship, even when they're not together. Have you ever had one of those fleeting moments when you can feel a connection and guess what someone you love may be doing? The phenomenon was a common occurrence for me. When I was traveling, despite the distance, I had a mind-body connection with Pat, a spiritual bond; I believe scientists call it "quantum consciousness." It's a profoundly complex subject beyond me, but I know it's real based on my experience.

## Popping the Question

After a few days away from Pat, the depth of love had become a revelation to me. All the dreams I thought I needed to pursue fell flat as I realized Pat was my prominent dream. I would gladly put everything in my life on hold just for her. I was determined to make her mine, and I wouldn't allow anything to get in the way. I had never experienced anything so intense before, which solidified my unwavering desire to make our relationship permanent. Though I knew it would take some time, I intended to marry Pat as soon as possible.

I decided to telephone her at the first opportunity while in Port Arthur on leave. The trouble was, there was no phone in her house; they shared the neighbor's phone. I made the call, the neighbor answered and I asked for Pat.

The neighbor promptly went next door and excitedly shouted, "Pat, someone in America on the phone!"

Pat entered the neighbor's living room to see the family of three sitting on the couch like birds perched on a wire. All eyes were staring at Pat in anticipation. I imagined they listened intently, especially the two women, sitting on the edge of their seats, smiling, ears tuned in and ready. They knew who I was and were very curious.

I was anxious to hear her voice again, imagine her smile as she spoke; her supervisor once said Pat was the best telephone operator the embassy ever had. Her tone was always crisp, cheery, pleasing to the ears, a voice with a built-in smile. The wait wasn't long; it seemed like hours but was only a few short minutes. Finally, Pat was on the phone.

"Lou?" she said.

I was delighted to hear her voice—especially at that moment in time.

"Of course, who else?"

She scoffed. "Silly, of course, I knew it was you. No one else would be calling from America! Where are you?"

"Home. In Port Arthur."

"How was the trip?"

"Okay, but I miss you."

Pat quietly sighed. Her short responses and pauses reminded me she was in her neighbor's house with eager ears listening to every word. She couldn't talk openly, but I wasn't calling only to chat I needed to propose to her there and then. It was not a temporary case of love and leave.

I took in a deep breath and said, "Let's get married."

On her end, a space of silence seemed like an eternity. My heart thumped.

She answered, "You're not kidding?"

"No. For real."

I felt awkward. We were apart for a while and maybe Pat had second thoughts. Talking to someone by telephone, you cannot see facial expressions, and you can't always know what someone is thinking just by the tone of voice. I couldn't tell whether Pat was smiling, frowning, or poker-faced. It was nerve-racking. I was afraid the proposal had shocked her—not the positive kind, but a shock of apprehension. I had expected and imagined she would be very excited, but what I heard was a bland, "You're not kidding?" On the other hand, I considered how many times she had said we would marry.

I said, "You don't sound too enthused."

Pat lowered her voice to a whisper. "I'm thrilled. It's just that, well, you know."

Those few words, and the way she said them, delivered to my mind and heart precisely what I needed to know—and what I had wanted to hear, longed to hear. The observant trio on the couch must have become even more curious, more immersed in the conversation now. Pat was only holding back because of nosey neighbors. I wished I had proposed to her personally. Perhaps I could at least see her eyes, but it had to be by telephone. It was a relief to know she was delighted, despite the awkward circumstances.

"I understand. You can't talk now. I'll call again to ask for your mom and dad's approval. And before we get married, I think you should come to America, spend some time here and see how you like it."

"Yes. Let's talk about it later."

We cut the call short, both of us saying a lot less than we wanted. My heart was soaring in the clouds. I felt like the luckiest man alive. I'm sure my marriage proposal wasn't a total surprise for Pat since she had predicted it would happen many times. Just the same, I knew she was excited — just as I was. A few days after the phone conversation, as promised, I called for Pat's dad Albert.

"Guess you heard. I want to marry your daughter."

"Okay by me, but you're a damn fool."

His tenor was a choppy, high-pitched Scottish brogue and his remarks temporarily took me aback.

He added, "She's just like her mother!"

We both laughed. I completely understood the Marshall humor extraordinaire. Judging from the time I had spent with Pat's mother, I could see how they were alike in disposition, spirit, beliefs and interests—which wasn't a bad thing.

Thoroughly excited, I contacted a friend at the State Department in Washington, D.C, the next day. I asked her to patch me into the switchboard at the American Embassy in London—directly to Pat. In those days, the public international phone service was minimal and unreliable, but going through the State Department was a shortcut, a direct, private line into the embassy. The phone system was the old upright PBX switchboards, a giant peg-board contraption with banana-type plugs at the end of flex cables. The operator plugged into a matrix of channels to connect incoming and outgoing calls within a telephone domain. My friend in D.C. patched me into the London embassy and within minutes, I heard Pat's cheerful voice.

"Good morning, American Embassy!"

It was good to hear her cheerful voice again! Next to Pat were four colleagues lined up in front of the switchboard in the telephone room. That didn't matter so much. They had earphones that prevented them from eavesdropping. Besides, they were friends of ours.

I said, "So, how's it going? Got your visa yet?"

That was a joke because, at that time, it took months to obtain a visa. There were stringent background checks, health examinations, the need for sponsorships and the list goes on.

"Still working on it!"

Pat had worked there some three years and there shouldn't have been any doubts. But that didn't matter to the authorities. Even though Pat had a security clearance, the embassy was strict about procedures.

"Well, tell them to expedite. I'm anxious for you to get over here!"

"Okay, I will. Should I get your Marine buddies to help convince them?"

I thought for a moment. "No, I don't think so. Those guys might get into more trouble than usual."

"Well, then, we'll have to go through the long process. Right?"

"Yeah, I guess so, and Sweetie, please keep me up to date."

Pat was temporarily interrupted by her supervisor. I suspected by a motion to cut off our conversation.

"Okay, will do. Gotta go now."

"Love you."

"Love you too."

The assurance Pat was obtaining a visa brought relief, excitement and a trace of apprehension. I thought maybe Pat had the jitters. Nonetheless, I felt better as we spoke and strengthened our relationship via phone calls and letters. It was a big step for both of us. Nonetheless, as time went on, I felt better as we spoke and strengthened our relationship via phone calls and letters. It was a big step for both of us.

Marriage was a life-changing decision—especially for her. It would mean moving to the States, living in a different culture, being away from her family and friends. Maybe it would take a while for her to assimilate. Or worse, get too homesick. I figured she'd adapt quickly, but the American lifestyle and culture differed from Britain in some ways. It was a significant move and I couldn't have blamed her if she was tense; but I figured she loved me and chances were, she would learn to enjoy living in America.

In my last few months in the Corps, I began thinking about the wedding. The thought of being married to Pat was exciting. I would not be coming to an empty home after work. I would soon fill my weekends with her company. I would introduce her to people, places and favorite things in America just as she had done for me in the U.K. The more I thought about married life, the more enthusiastic I became.

Before leaving Pendleton, I had saved up enough money to buy an engagement ring at the P.X. I had already planned everything, at least in a general way. After mustering out of the Corps, I would temporarily live with my brother Nick and his family in Bellville, Illinois. I would get a job and earn some money while waiting for Pat's arrival at the St. Louis airport. I knew getting her visa would be the longest part of the plan. Security was tighter than ever and visa processing took longer than usual. Though the American Embassy had cleared Pat to work there for several years, she still had to undergo a police background check and a strict physical exam, as well as fulfilling a long list of other prerequisites before she could live here.

# Chapter Ten

## Storm Clouds Coming, Brighter Days Ahead

A ll went according to plan, at least for a while. Once settled into my brother's house, I went to work as a clerk in a highway toll office. I also played gigs in St. Louis. After a long and agonizing wait, everything finally started coming together with Pat's visa and her trip. We would soon be together again! Our relationship would resume and plans for a new, exciting future would be underway. My excitement increased a few notches each day. It was a fresh beginning, a new journey.

Since Pat had that unique gift of intuition, she predicted our marriage long before it was on my radar. In contrast, I relied on logical thinking and facts to imagine the future. If I'd had the kind of insight Pat had, I might have felt the impending trouble in front of us.

A few days before Pat's flight, I received a phone call from her dad. I expected to hear nothing but good news. What Albert said to me was the exact opposite. Pat had been in an auto accident and was in the hospital. In the sudden stress, I pressed the phone hard to my ear. His words echoed painfully loud and clear.

**Tragedy and Hope**

"No. It can't be."

"Afraid so." He said in a sad tone.

I sucked in a breath as his words sunk in. My heart skipped a beat. A glut of questions flashed through my mind.

"What happened?"

"She was riding home with a friend and they hit a bridge."

"How bad is it?"

"She's in the hospital with a head and leg injury."

My thoughts went haywire, visualizing Pat in hospital. I had to book a flight immediately. The image of Pat lying in a hospital bed plagued my mind: an oxygen mask, needles and tubes, and intravenous feeding.

I tried to be positive, or maybe it was just denial, but I refused to consider worst-case scenarios. I slowly began to convince myself that Pat would be okay. That calmed me a bit and helped me to collect myself.

"I'm coming over," I said.

"Right. I'll tell Pat. Let us know when."

"I'll call you as soon as I book a flight."

As the heart-wrenching call ended, I stood motionless, cradling the phone's receiver. The word "accident" reverberated in my mind like a gunshot in an echo chamber. I was stunned; my world had stopped. Nick urged me to tell them what was wrong, but for a moment, I was speechless. I finally gathered myself enough to explain what had happened. I felt enveloped by a dark cloud, cruelly interrupting my happy dream.

My world had suddenly gone from joy and excitement to disaster and anguish. The harsh reality is life doesn't always go according to plan. One minute you're soaring in the clouds. The next minute, you're kicked in the gut and slammed to the ground with broken bones and broken hopes.

I wondered why this was happening. We'd been ready to start planning the wedding and our future together. Instead, Pat was lying in a hospital, in what condition only God knew. My heart contracted painfully at such morbid thoughts. Forcing myself to snap out of the gloom, I immediately checked flights to London. I had saved enough money to pay for a round-trip plane ticket.

Within a few days, I was in the air heading to London. I focused my thoughts on how serious Pat's injuries were throughout the flight. Albert gave me more information—it was still a touch-and-go situation. I tried to avoid pondering worst-case scenarios, but my mind vacillated between hope and despair.

I managed to reject most negative thoughts. I convinced myself this would be nothing more than a temporary setback. We'd had a beautiful courtship—our minds, hearts and personalities had always fit together like pieces in a puzzle. Our destiny was to be together and nothing could tear us apart, not even tragedy.

## Back at Pat's side

My flight to the U.K. was mentally torturous. I didn't know what to expect. After landing at Heathrow Airport, I hurried through the hassle of taking trains and taxicabs to Pat's home in Corby, hours away from Heathrow Airport. When I arrived, Albert and Lovey informed me that Pat was improving and gave me more background on what had happened.

After leaving the U.K., Pat started working for American Express at an RAF base under U.S. control in Alconbury, England, about 68 miles north of London and a 30-mile drive from Corby. A group of fellow workers at the office had held a going-away party for Pat. Afterward, a friend would drive her home.

When they were rounding a sharp bend in the narrow road, crossing a creek, the car hit the bridge abutment. Their evening filled with fun had turned disastrous. The impact threw Pat head-first into the windshield and gave her a concussion. She also had broken ribs and a leg injury.

When Pat's dad and I arrived at the hospital, she was lying in a bed in a large barracks-style, open room. There was no privacy. It was a large room with a row of beds on each side. Private rooms in most hospitals under nationalized health care were rare or nonexistent. My heart dropped when I saw a thick layer of gauze wrapped around Pat's head and her leg in a cast. Pat looked embarrassed. I felt like an oaf, standing there, painfully staring at her. She gave me a weak smile. At a glance, I could see she felt humiliated and sad because the accident had scuttled our plans.

Regardless of her distressing predicament, she was still beautiful to me, no matter her condition or the circumstances. I wanted to hold her, kiss her, but could only stand next to her, talk and hold her hand. She was helpless and quiet, unable to say much about the turn of events. Understandably, her movements were slow and she seemed exhausted. She'd survived a car accident and was still weak from the surgery. A cloud of sadness came over me.

A week later, Pat was at home on crutches, on the road to recovery. The doctors said it would take at least six weeks to heal. While she slowly recovered, I hoped to get a job at an auto body shop. My limited experience doing auto body work in Texas and California was enough to snare a job offer. Still, Corby's shop manager said he could hire me only if I had a work visa. I inquired about a permit but was not qualified. Besides, unemployment was high and a foreigner getting a work visa was not likely.

I often wonder what would have happened if I'd found a job there. I might have stayed in the U.K. for years, perhaps even the rest of my life. I enjoyed the lifestyle and I could have obtained a good education there. Some Americans stationed in England, including Embassy Marines, married local girls and became British citizens.

Despite the tight quarters, we got along fine. During Pat's rehabilitation, I realized that Pat inherited her vibrant personality and sharp humor. Her family didn't often let earthly things dampen their spirit. Their optimism was rock solid. They carried on with everything despite the circumstances.


## Leaving Home is Hard

After Pat fully recovered from her injuries, we boarded a plane bound for the U.S. She had been mostly silent during the long taxi ride from Corby to London. But I understood and shrugged it off.

As the plane was leveling at cruising altitude, Pat began to sob. Understandably, it was a pivotal experience to leave her family and friends. She was moving thousands of miles away from home—something I'm sure she never dreamed of doing before she met me. I tried to calm her down but couldn't help her much—it required a woman's touch. Thank God for a compassionate flight attendant who comforted Pat during the long flight. I had high hopes that her trial period in the States would expose any significant issues before we became committed to marriage. I didn't know how she would handle being away from her family, and though it concerned me, I clung to the hope and belief that our deep love for each other would carry us through.

Meanwhile, winter had hit the St. Louis area. We landed at the airport, retrieved our luggage and went through the automatic doors. We faced a gust of freezing wind and a mountain of snow piled up on both sides of the walkway. We found our way to the car, which had no heater—an item I had forgotten. It came off the assembly line for California weather and there was no need for a heater.

It was a long and brutal 20-mile drive back to my brother's house— cold, snowy, wet and icy like Siberian weather. Fingers, toes, nose, ears, all extremities felt frozen. Every few minutes, the windshield accumulated a thick layer of ice and I couldn't see the road well, so we had to stop often to scrape it clean. Shivering cold and chattering teeth took on a new meaning. We rolled the windows down at one point, thinking it would help keep the windshield clear. But the wind and snowy mist quickly became overwhelming.

Fortunately, I had stowed a blanket and a towel in the back seat and Pat was wearing a heavy coat. I wrapped the towel around my head, covering my ears, with the blanket wrapped around my torso. I looked like a clownish mummy. Pat looked at me, held back a giggle and then we couldn't stop laughing. When we finally arrived at the house, my hands and feet were numb. But a little soaking in luke-warm water did the trick.

## Humor Outshines Adversity

The fiasco should have made a horrible first impression on Pat, but she took it in stride as always. We laughed the whole way to the house—and this was indicative of how Pat would endure and thrive in America. She could find comedy in almost any situation; nothing seemed to diminish her ability to make light of things. When I was angry over something, a slow grin would appear on her face, which defused the conflict and sparked a burst of laughter.

Pat demonstrated a positive outlook that I eventually learned to emulate. Though I could never reach her buoyancy level, through her, it was better not to take life too seriously and insert a grain of comedy whatever the circumstances. She would often play the witty comic role. And she was very good at one-liners. Sometimes when I said, "I'll be back," she would respond with, "Thanks for the warning!" Pat's happy persona was witty and contagious. Whenever I saw her smiling face, heard her voice and looked into her eyes, my heart leaped for joy. Her beautiful spirit was with me again.

After a few weeks in Bellville, we bundled up, got back in the no-heater car, and took off for Port Arthur. We meandered from Illinois through Missouri and Arkansas, down to Texas. On the way, we stopped at a restaurant in Little Rock, where a couple of state police were in a nearby booth having breakfast.

Fixing her eyes on their holstered Glock pistols, Pat cupped her hand over her mouth and whispered, "Look. Real guns. Just like in the movies!"

I laughed. "Yes, and with live ammo!"

Our road trip gave her a taste of Americana—southern style. Pat's enthusiasm made me more excited than ever for the future. She was enjoying her new world, and I was genuinely thrilled for her—for us —as I saw the dark effects of her tragic accident and the trauma of leaving her family fading.

## Back in Texas

Six months before our wedding, Pat settled at my family home in Pear Ridge. She was quick to assimilate into our culture, my family and friends. Meanwhile, I was diligently looking for work—any work to earn money. We paid for the wedding and more. I had spent what meager savings I had going back to England during Pat's recovery.

Jobs were still scarce in Port Arthur and I worked as a collector for a furniture store.

I spent most of my time driving out to the "projects," where low-income people and dead-beats lived in public housing units. The store sold to anyone who could make a down payment and sign "X" for the purchase. After that, it was my job to collect monthly payments. I developed a particular routine that worked well: I would call welfare recipients and tell them, "Sit on your check until I get there." It was a way to upstage other collectors. I'd get there fast and cash the person's welfare check, minus the payment due.

That strategy paid off; by three months or so before the wedding, we had enough money to rent a place to live. We found a small, cozy garage apartment—a one-bedroom apartment over the garage in the upscale Griffing Park neighborhood, the wealthy section near Pear Ridge. The homes in Griffing Park were large, mansion-like, big yards and majestic oak trees with low-lying limbs adorning the landscape. Years before, this is where Dad and I mowed grass when union workers at the refinery went on strike.

The apartment was like a studio apartment, with a bedroom, a sitting area and a small kitchen. The place fit our budget and the owners were ultra-nice people. Griffing Park used to be a standalone city until Port Arthur annexed it in 1983. Located on the other side of the train tracks where I used to play, it reminded me of my years as a youth. Settling into the garage apartment brought back many memories, most of which I shared with Pat.

When I was eight years old, we had moved from our modest house on 10th street in downtown Port Arthur out to Pear Ridge, a rural community on the north end of town. Our new home was a modest three-bedroom, clapboard farmhouse with a barn and a chicken coup at 29th Street and 9th Avenue. Previous owners had converted a maid's quarters into a detached garage. They also added a screened-in back porch and a bathroom with a commode, sink and vintage clawfoot bathtub. There was a lot more open space in Pear Ridge than we'd known in the city, which meant a simpler lifestyle. We could walk just a few blocks and go hunting or fishing. The lot next to our barn was a worn baseball diamond also used by the neighborhood for sandlot football, volleyball, etc.

When Dad's union was on strike at the refinery, there was little money. To earn some cash and help the family in those times, we cut grass in Griffing Park, on the other side of the railroad tracks. Sometimes we'd have to mow a whole acre of thick grass with a push-mower. That chore wasn't so bad; the feel of prickly, tall St. Augustine grass under your bare feet is unforgettable. Energy drinks? There was no such thing back then. We ate pecans, pears and juicy purple Texas Everbearing Figs from trees in our yard for energy. Downing these snacks with an old-fashioned small bottle of Coca-Cola from the corner drug store was our "energy drink." It provided a slight boost needed, especially on the hot days of summer.

# Chapter Eleven

## Crystal Beach

Flash-forward to the present. I'm back on the second deck of the beach house at Crystal Beach, ruminating, slipping deeper into the back roads of memory. I'm staring down at the driveway, just yards from the sandy beach entrance. The moist Gulf breeze, about 10 knots, is steady out of the south. Today is perfect weather for enjoying the best part of the Gulf Coast: the long, narrow Bolivar Peninsula, across the channel from Galveston Island —coastlines on each side, the whole peninsula just 42 square miles in size. It's early June, with summer almost upon us. We can expect mostly sunny days and hot temperatures in Southeast Texas.

The Gulf waves are rolling in. Chalk-white, foamy crests blanket the beach. I scan the beach and see an assortment of golf carts passing by, sporting the stars and stripes and the Lone Star flag of Texas, one of many flags this state has flown during its history. A woman slowly paces the sand with her head craned down, searching for seashells, shark teeth, marine memorabilia. A father and two sons, waist-deep in water, fish with a rod and reel. He turns and shouts to his wife on the beach.

"Take a picture!"

Meanwhile, a cluster of Great Blue Herons flies overhead in a slow, majestic formation, navigating east to west. To my left, a bird regally perched nearby on a telephone pole takes off and glides a few feet in front of me, proving its identity—a Laughing Gull—so named because its call mimics laughter. Beachcombers, anglers, families, sunbathers and many seafowls inhabit the Gulf shore.

Undeniably, people-watching, bird-watching, sunbathing and the subtle crashing of waves on the beach combine to create an atmosphere for rest, relaxation and contemplation. I tilt my head back, fix my gaze beyond the haze, wondering if Pat is looking down at me. I'm momentarily mesmerized, a hopeless sentimentalist stepping into the twilight zone, wondering about the afterlife.

I hear a knock on the front door. I stroll down to the first landing and meet up with a local handyman tasked to work on the house. A lean Native American, he speaks with the native Southeast Texas drawl I used to have. He briefs me on his project and somewhere in our conversation, he mentions "jeep weekend." Better known as "topless weekend." It's an event where thousands of jeep lovers gather and troll with loud, buzz-thumping sub-woofers quivering the ground.

I ask, "Topless? You mean topless jeeps or women?"

"Both. Jeeps and women."

He feigns peeling off his T-shirt. "Like the Mardi Gras in New Orleans. It can get wild and crazy, especially at night."

That was surprising since Crystal Beach is a staid, family-oriented, mature community with expensive well-kept homes, a very trendy vacation spot for surrounding communities. How times have changed. It wasn't much like that when Bo and I spent hours on end as teenage beach-bums on the prowl.

I began to think about the good times Bo and I had at McFaddin Beach, which is toward Sabine Pass—the nights sitting around a campfire with our dates roasting marshmallows. We had some good times back in the "Happy Days" era. A starry sky above and the rolling, crashing waves at the beach made for romantic, carefree moments as we listened to good music. Thank God for KPAC radio in Port Arthur and radio station KTRM in Beaumont—emceed by J.P. Richardson, the "Big Bopper" of *Chantilly Lace* fame. These stations provided Top 40 music, the Rock 'n Roll era's birth, when the lyrics, the rhythm, the melodies made sense. And the music was uplifting. We took advantage of our youth, our crude boldness, and the mesmerizing beach.

## Reverie and Reminiscence

It's been six weeks since my last stay on the Bolivar Peninsula. Time for another round of writing. It's a Wednesday. After maneuvering through Galveston, waiting for the boat wasn't as bad as it would have been on the weekend when people scrambled towards the Gulf coast, then bottleneck at the ferry Galveston side. Still, a thirty-minute wait time added to over an hour of driving was boring. I snacked on an energy bar—you learn to prepare for such events and expect delays at specific points in your journey. Once on the ferry, I emerged from my truck, went over and leaned on the bulkhead railing, enjoying the brisk breeze and thinking of times with Pat. Same area, same setting, but Pat is not with me.

I'm facing reality again. I fall into sadness, but it quickly passes. My mind switches to the beach house on the Bolivar side, another 5 minutes away—a straight shot on Highway 87, about 3 miles. To get there from Galveston, you have to ride the ferry. From the east side, from Port Arthur, you go to Winnie on I-10, then down to High Island and using 87, about 36 miles.

The ferry glides smoothly over choppy water with ease. The ferry captain navigates the channel with no problem. However, a snarl of ship traffic sometimes complicates his repetitive, boring trip between Galveston and Bolivar. Before long, the ferry is approaching the Bolivar landing dock. I hop into my '04 Dodge Ram truck, but I wait until I'm ready to roll before starting the engine—a six-cylinder, 24-valve Cummins Turbo Diesel, one of the best motors made. And it's loud. So loud, it sounds like a B-25 bomber on a sortie. The noise disturbs people, especially in close confines. One day in Houston, I was driving down a narrow tunnel in an indoor parking garage. Noise from the 4-inch exhaust pipe bounced off the cement walls, sound waves colliding, scaling up high in volume. When I rounded the last corner, approaching the automatic kiosk to pay, an attendant was standing next to it, posing a toothy smile. I could see he wanted to talk. I pulled up next to him and lowered my window.

He chuckled and said, "I *had* to see what was coming down the tunnel!"

I laughed. "Yeah, I know."

Approaching the Bolivar landing site, the ferry slows, yaws sideways, shifts straight and meets the landing with a tender bump. After exiting on the Bolivar side, I continue down the two-lane highway towards the beach community. Highway 87 runs the peninsula's length, with roads branching off to the north and south towards clusters of stilted homes along the coastlines.

On the way, I slow down, look to the north and gawk at the iconic, blackened Point Bolivar Lighthouse jutting in the sky. For some reason, lighthouses intrigue me. I often wonder what it would be like to live in or next to one, but it's only a fantasy. I don't think I could stand being isolated, living like a hermit for long. As much as I've avoided crowds and shunned networking in my business life, I've eventually come to enjoy meeting new people, having lively, fresh conversations. I believe I get that from Dad, who was cheerful and friendly. He socialized with people a lot; his immigrant persona never stopped him from being gregarious and outgoing, at least most of the time.

The following day, I sip my Seaport coffee on the sun deck, the ideal treatment for a late night of writing. Here I can let loose of stress, erase tension, let my mind wander. The serenity triggers memories of events in the past, specifically a scene when Pat and I were at the Galveston beach on a hot, sweltering day before our marriage. I should've known better than to let her stay in the sun so long, with her fair, milky skin. Her innocent eagerness and my not thinking came with a price. We were thoroughly enjoying the beach. Pat was splashing about in the water, then laying out to dry on an oversized towel under a small umbrella propped at an angle in the sand.

Unfortunately, she had quite a bad sunburn; she had turned strawberry-red. When we got home, Pat went from feeling faint and dehydrated to becoming extraordinarily ill and vomiting. I was alarmed at Pat's condition. She appeared to have suffered a heat stroke. Leaning over her, I held a towel of ice cubes to her forehead, then around her neck and trickled cold water on her face. Of course, Pat, being a trooper, bounced back and recovered quickly. She was one tough lassie, a survivor able to adapt and overcome any situation. She had left her home, moved to America and made a life here.

# Chapter Twelve

## Texas Welcome

Pat had no trouble blending with my family; she immediately became one of us. Upon her arrival in Port Arthur, everyone treated her like a celebrity of sorts, an ambassador from England with an eloquent accent. Everyone immediately accepted her, especially my younger sisters Sandra and Mary. They thought Pat was chic and they loved her bubbly personality. The minute she stepped inside our house, Mom immediately asked Pat, "Are you hungry? I'll fix you something to eat."

"No, thank you. I'm not hungry."

Pat glanced my way with a quizzical expression. I chuckled and said, "It's an Italian thing. You don't have to eat."

Pat's accent intrigued everyone, and likewise, Pat loved Dad's Sicilian dialect. She and Dad got along incredibly well; they shared a sense of humor. He teased her by calling her "Pat Marshallo."

Pat would laugh and say, "No, no. It's 'Marr-shole.'"

Dad would slap his knee and burst out laughing. He was a cheerful man and a good match for Pat. It was a battle of wits between the two. Dad baited Pat with wittiness and loved her quick, adept responses.

Pat would often help mom in the kitchen, where she learned to cook our family recipe for spaghetti sauce—or in Italian terms, "gravy." It was relatively simple to make, but there was a distinct process. After developing the gravy mix (fried tomato paste, sautéed garlic, onions and bell peppers), we prepared a stuffed, seared pork roast, then added the roast to a pot of water and broth. We let it simmer awhile, adding spices and stirring until it reached the desired thickness. Spaghetti with red sauce was a traditional Sunday meal. Pat loyally continued this tradition, making the meal on Sundays and holidays.

* * *

Things were progressing well, settling in the U.S. and pursuing our plans. It felt good being back with family and friends, the old gang. Once I started receiving a steady paycheck, we could rent the furnished garage apartment on the edge of Griffing Park. Not surprisingly, Pat didn't have a problem finding a job. She went to work for the First National Bank on Procter Street. Pat was a talented employee who was very diplomatic with people; she got along well with everyone at the bank and became instantly popular wherever she went. Her rare innocent simplicity was infectious. She was an expert at breaking the ice and establishing common ground with everyone. She was a superb customer service person, able to soothe emotions and go directly to solving a problem—a person of empathy and action.

Wherever Pat was, there was humor. And the difference between our southern dialect, mores, and the King's English made for humorous situations. Pat and her co-workers ordered hamburgers from a local restaurant one day at her office.

Pat gave an order: "I'll have lettuce, tomatoes, pickles, mustard and cut-up the onions."

Someone asked, "Why did you say, 'cut-up the onions'?"

"Because I want them chopped up," she answered. "You know, . . . 'Cut the onions.'"

Everyone cracked up. Pat shrugged, then burst out laughing. But she didn't understand what was funny until someone explained *"without onions"* in the local colloquium.

While in Port Arthur, we formed a small band—a quartet—and performed at different venues.

Pat became a big hit. One evening, Pat was the vocalist with a big band—Harry Vaughn's Orchestra—at the Thomas Jefferson high school prom. When Pat sang, the students were so impressed they stopped dancing and gathered in front of the stage. My chest swelled with pride.

We often went to the amusement center on Pleasure Island, an island formed by the Corps of Engineers when they dredged to create the Port Arthur Canal in 1899 and the Sabine Neches Intra-coastal Waterway in 1908. The island is adjacent to Sabine Lake, off the Gulf of Mexico. The amusement park was on the meandering Sabine-Neches Canal on the lakeside, separating Pleasure Island from Port Arthur. The place was a favorite destination for young lovers to park under a bright moon with sparkles reflecting off crested waves. Cars with boy-girl figures behind foggy windows fringed the seawall. Radios cranking out the latest hits of the '50s, while a steady warm breeze off the Gulf added to the mood and made for a romantic setting. It was the perfect oasis for young adults.

Pat and I would often go to Pleasure Island, talk about our future, dream of a home and raising a family. The conversation usually started with Pat's tongue-in-cheek remark, "I always knew we would marry."

We occasionally double-dated with one of my buddies and a girl-friend. We usually parked at the far end, near the ballroom, where dreamy music often echoed across a placid lakeshore. The moon hovered over the Texas horizon like a giant yellowish-orange balloon. Stars sparkled like psychedelic diamonds against a deep blue celestial curtain. The turbulent waves splashed against the granite wall, and the moon-lit spray of droplets on the windshield glistened like multiple pin lights.

It was best to keep track of time on the island because the drawbridge was shut down at night, leaving its claws open high in the air until early morning. After a romantic evening on Pleasure Island, a class-mate friend and his fiancé were trapped on the island until five o'clock the following day. They had some explaining to do that day.

By far, our favorite spot for serene privacy was on the levee above the canal. We often parked our Chevy at the levee along the canal. On a clear night, we would stare at the starry sky above the horizon. It was our special refuge, a unique ambiance, much like our spot in Grosvenor Square Park, London, a place for tranquil togetherness. As the years rolled on, that old Chevy at the levee became for us a symbolic remembrance of our love and dreams, a happy time in Port Arthur. During our engagement, I painted *Pat & Lou* on the glove compartment in cursive, a sort of '50s art deco style.

On the levee, you can easily watch the oil tankers gracefully glide through the water just yards away from the granite seawall. It's mesmerizing to watch and hear the vessels slicing the water, creating bands of rolling waves. It's an excellent place for reflection and soli-tude. It was springtime, the perfect weather to have a picnic. Our spot was at the end of fashionable Seawall Drive on a levee next to Rose Hill Manor, a historic landmark. The elegant 6,000-square-foot mansion, constructed in 1906, had been the home of a banker and former mayor of Port Arthur, Rome Hatch Woodworth. His family later bequeathed the stately house to the city of Port Arthur, including funding to support the property. It now serves as a popular venue for special events, such as weddings, business meetings and private parties.

## A Bachelor's Last Stand

We often made the "drag" westward on Procter Street to downtown. Turning left in front of the train station, we'd enter Seawall Drive, which parallels the canal, on the way to Rose Hill Manor. One day, we parked the car next to the levee, gathered our picnic stuff and hiked up the slope to the crest of the levee. We placed our picnic basket on a blanket spread across the thick grass and sat shoulder-to-shoulder, enjoying a gentle, moist air current wafting off Lake Sabine from across the canal.

"What a beautiful day!" Pat said. "Sunshine, clear skies, not too hot."

She turned and pointed at the drawbridge a few miles away; it was often open for ships, each section vertical, pointing to the heavens.

"The ship under the bridge. What kind is it?"

"An oil tanker. A pretty big one too. Probably going to the docks up around Port Neches."

We would watch the roughly 1,500-foot tanker pass under the bridge and glide through the narrow canal past us. The spinning vortices in the wake of the ship would splash against the massive granite blocks rimming the channel. Volleys of mist would spray towards us, bathing our faces with refreshing coolness. Pat would wave eagerly at the crew on deck and they would wave back.

During our engagement, life in Port Arthur was a good test for compatibility and Pat's willingness to live in America. It seemed a good fit for her and all who knew her. Pat embraced the lifestyle of Americana and our band of friends. Wherever she went, she made friends. She still missed her home country from time to time; we expected that and we made sure to plan regular visits. But Pat was surrounded by people who loved her, which helped lessen her home-sickness. Her charming personality and engaging optimism deeply affected everyone. People quickly sensed her sincerity and honest, unpretentious character. She *loved* people without expecting anything in return, as we should all do. For most people, it's pretty tricky. But for Pat, love was a natural characteristic.

She also had a comforting aura around her. In impromptu meetings with strangers, they would tell her their life story, or at least a dramatic snippet of it, something that beckoned an understanding and sympathetic response. Once, while waiting for her in the super-market parking lot, I noticed Pat talking to a man for several minutes while waiting in line at the checkout counter.

When she returned to the car, I asked, "So, what's his story?"

"Well, he's divorced, his son is on drugs, his mother is in hospital and he lost his job."

"He said all that in a few minutes?"

I'd had a good idea of what was coming, but I was still shocked by the array of details a stranger would give. It was uncanny how people would spill out their deepest secrets to her. Although I knew her perceptive abilities very well, I had a hard time understanding them. She had something special, a deep-seated, intuitive nature.

She nodded. "Feel sorry for him."

Pat often speckled our lives with fun surprises, and she was good at it. She would catch me off guard with her playful antics. Sometimes she could be aggressive, but in a funny way that often left us howling with laughter.

At one point, I began distinguishing love from romance. Romance or passion is a human obsession, perhaps fleeting and temporary. But Pat and I fell into a deep-rooted love during our courtship, a love that continually grew over time. Although passion and love naturally blend, true love goes beyond simple romance. A life-long, holistic connection between us was evolving into a constant reality and the big day of the wedding was near.

* * *

The bachelor party had been wild and crazy but I survived unscathed. From the start, it was a complete surprise. Bo had asked me to go with him to check out some beach real estate, but he first had to, "Stop at Jim Mac's house." We went straight to Jim's back porch, where a group of rowdy guys surrounded a keg of beer. The scene wasn't unusual, but why didn't I know about it?

Then Snake chuckled and said, "Hey man, this is your party! Have a beer!"

The party lasted throughout the night, but I didn't stay the course—as time went by, it got crazy—very crazy. At one point, I had to fight off five guys who tried to douse my privates with Silver Nitrate—a chemical absconded from a chemical plant by "Moose" Mouton another member of our group. They had me on top of a car, wrestling with the pranksters. If they had succeeded, the stuff would have turned my skin black. Not to mention the injury it might have caused. If it touches your skin, it takes a long time to return to its natural color. Like a wild man, I punched, kicked and did whatever I could to get the guys off. They eventually gave up and, with a few bruises, went back into the house. Next was the wedding!

# Chapter Thirteen

## The Wedding

It was the long-awaited, thrilling phase of our relationship. We underwent a long, sometimes arduous journey to reach this most climactic occasion, and the months before the wedding were hectic. Time spent apart, Pat's accident, saving money for the wedding, living on a shoestring budget—the setbacks were sometimes exhausting, but everything went well.

Of course, Pat took everything in stride. She viewed problems through a different lens; that is, problems turned inside out were opportunities in some shape or form. And in our case, overcoming obstacles together strengthened our relationship, which made a lot of sense. If anyone could see things through her eyes, a vast majority of worries would be for naught.

We saved enough to pay for nearly everything, including Pat's dress and the wedding. Unfortunately, Pat's dad Albert, could not be there. Moose would be the stand-in to give Pat as my bride. The presence of Pat's mother, Lovey and Pat's sister Jackie and her husband John put a touch of extra icing on our elegant triple layer cake with a husband/wife figurine on top. It wasn't a fancy, expensive wedding, but still refined enough to please about 150 guests. We made sure the U.K. delegation would be comfortable and enjoy themselves thoroughly. And as expected, they did. They felt fully welcomed and approved of Pat's new family and circle of friends.

Before the service began, my schoolmate Johnny (Preston) Courville sang the processional song, *Ave Maria*, and it brought tears to many eyes. The time had come and yet I was in la-la land. My best man, Bo, Moose, and I were in the front pew, waiting for the priest's cue. When he signaled, I was not paying attention. Moose prompted me with a low grunt and a sharp elbow jab in my ribs. That sprang me awake. It was the grand moment—a huge turning point. Moose went to join Pat as Bo, and I made our way to the foot of the altar and stood with the Monsignor. All eyes turned towards the back of the church as we waited for the procession. Following tradition, the ushers and bridesmaids walked down the aisle first, followed by Moose and Pat.

The Monsignor conducted the event at St. Mary's Church on July 27th, 1963. The church was old-style architecture with a high ceiling. The sun penetrated the stain-glass windows and washed the church with a collage of multiple colors.

Since we knew that this would be a once-in-a-lifetime thing, we tried to make it as memorable as possible. The church wedding was a beautiful, well-executed ceremony. We would've liked a bagpiper but could not afford the cost (years later, we had a bagpiper at our daughter Angela's wedding). We could not wait to start life officially as husband and wife. Everything else quickly vanished when I looked down that long aisle and saw her. Pat seemed like an angel dressed in a flowing, bright white dress. She was stunningly beautiful, luminous and alluring. I suppose every groom has a similar experience, but I felt mine was extra special. My eyes slightly teared up at the sight of the most astonishingly lovely person anyone could imagine.

Bridesmaids wore violet outfits with mauve and white rose bouquets and Pat held mauve, pink and cream roses. What is vivid is the image of a tiered cathedral-length veil over Pat's glowing face. It couldn't hide her bright smile, as enticing as a starburst. I became intensely aware of my surroundings and what was about to happen as she became the sole center of my attention. Her hair, gown, the graceful walk down the aisle and a hint of happiness and nervousness in her eyes created a permanent portrait in my mind. My disorientation vanished as I stood before her at attention, dressed in a traditional black tuxedo, my spine ramrod straight and my face a beaming smile. All I could think was, how do I rate someone like her? How did I get so lucky to have someone this beautiful, this loveable? God blessed me with a woman like her, someone who encouraged quality of life over all else. That's how I saw her on our wedding day: the perfect woman in the world.

Following the grand processional to the front of the church, Moose "gave" Pat to me. Bo solemnly stood next to me for the song, the Biblical readings and Monsignor's short sermon about matrimony, one of the seven sacraments of God's grace in the Catholic religion. We took our vows and exchanged rings. Then, finally, it was time to kiss Pat—a short but affectionate one. After Monsignor introduced us as "man and wife," we were officially together in mind and spirit and we felt the phenomenon, fully and deeply. At last, Pat was mine and I was hers—we officially belonged to each other in a bond of love and marital commitment.

## Celebrating the Beauty of Love

Outside the church, the crowd showered us with rice and hoopla. The reception, held at the National Maritime union hall, was a down-home, fun-filled event. Pat was excited and delighted to be at the center of such a wonderful time in our lives. Our marriage was the beginning of a lifelong commitment. Naturally, she took on her role as the consummate host and played it to perfection. Tom Donegan, a friend of Irish descent, was the union's chapter president and he made the arrangements. His wife Mary was directly from Ireland and we socialized often. Tom let us use the union hall and rounded up local business sponsors for a great food layout. A Wurlitzer jukebox provided our favorite Pop-Rock tunes, ideal for inspiration and dancing. The main thing we supplied was a keg of beer, which Snake gladly attended the whole evening. The music was good, the fellowship great, we had plenty of food and a wedding cake for everyone. And, way more than anything else, Pat and I embraced the awareness that we had entered something beautiful.

Everyone, especially Pat's family, had a great time, even the photographer, who didn't want to leave. Surprisingly, the photographer was Snake's prime beer-drinking contender. He was a strait-laced fellow, a bit of a homebody by all indications. Within a few hours, he was amply excited and a very active participant in the reception. Expecting him to be home at the time, his wife called.

She said, "Where are you?"

In trouble was where he was! But he did his job well and decided to stay for the whole thing. Pat's family could readily see how nicely she fit in and how much everyone loved her. They also recognized Pat's spunk and humor had captivated everyone, especially Bo, the master jester. He was the blue-eyed Cajun Fonzie in our group. At just a little over five-foot, about 125 pounds, he was an accomplished athlete, aggressive as a Tasmanian devil and had a penchant for mischief.

Bo and Pat hit it off. Pat appreciated the same sense of humor as Bo and our group. Pat and Bo would try to outwit each other at every opportunity. They would tease each other, both trying to get in the last word. Pat was usually the victor, but Bo stubbornly refused to admit defeat. He would try to come back with a witty answer that would lead to another playful battle. It was refreshing to see Pat respond to Bo's humor and at times, his arrogance. But it wasn't surprising—that was Pat's game too—she loved to banter. And she never got tired of sitting for hours laughing heartily as my group recalled stories of our shenanigans, many of which occurred at funerals where Bo, Mikey Rosetta, Lloyd Monceaux and I occasionally worked aside from the ambulance service. Coffins and embalming rooms were perfect sites for ghostly pranks.

The reception was an event to behold. Cajuns, Scots, Irish and old country Italians joined together in our world of Southeast Texas, an incredible mix of four cultures—an occasion of lasting sentimental value. Pat's jovial relatives fit in with the crowd nicely. Their energetic dancing, conversation and cheerfulness made for a lively bunch. Everyone was impressed by their down-to-earth personality and mannerisms. And my gang of friends eagerly stirred up the fun. Jim assumed the role of self-designated escort to keep Lovey busy dancing, circulating in the crowd. The Scots are well into country dance bands, upbeat music, dancing and celebrating a marriage with customs in wedding receptions. Understandably, one tradition, the "Blackening" of the groom, is no longer practiced. It involves stripping the groom and covering him with treacle and flour or feathers. Luckily, the rascals at my bachelor party knew nothing of this. Otherwise, I'm sure they would have continued with the Sulphur Nitrate treatment!

The reception was a blast and our honeymoon was economy class. The reception was a remarkable event for a lot of people. Bo had a flashy, Cherry red, '51 Chevrolet Impala convertible with red leather upholstery, so I used it as my honeymoon car. Bo had dutifully washed and waxed it for the occasion. As tradition goes, he had tied tin cans to the back bumper but fell short of putting any signs such as "Just Married" on his prize car, not even fingerprints.

As we were about ready to drive off with tin cans tied to the back bumper, Bo shouted, "Don't get it dirty. I just waxed it!"

I chuckled and said, "See you in a few months. Use my car!"

We drove off amid fanfare. After a few blocks, I removed the tin cans and we headed towards Beaumont, less than 20 miles away.

## Starting Life Together

We checked into a mid-range motel, had dinner and went to a movie theater to watch the movie "Bye Bye Birdie." Following our low-budget honeymoon in Beaumont, we both had a craving for Mom's Sunday dinner, so we checked out of the motel and headed back to Pear Ridge. It was a delight having the family together to celebrate our marriage. Afterward, we headed to the garage apartment, our first habitat near Griffing Park. The next day, a Monday, it was back to work. It was a short, simple, low-cost honeymoon, but it followed an unforgettable wedding. People have talked about the reception for many years.

A few months after the wedding, Pat and I decided to move to the Washington, D.C., area. I got in touch with my Marine buddy in London, Jerry Cramer. He and his wife Diane had settled there after Jerry left the Corps. Diane was still with the State Department and Jerry worked for an investment firm. They gave us the heads-up on the D.C. scenario. Job opportunities and several colleges offered attractive prospects for building our careers. We saw it as a step in the right direction.

Meanwhile, we maintained a thrifty lifestyle to save money before moving. Pat was still with the First National Bank and I continued with the furniture store in Port Arthur. It would be several months before we could leave for D.C. and we made the most of socializing with family and friends. A few months after the wedding, Pat's mom Lovey arrived from the U.K. to visit for a couple of weeks. As one can imagine, having her daughter just married and living in a country thousands of miles away had to be emotionally complicated. Deep in my heart, I felt the anxiety they both endured. They were very close.

I consciously made a vow to manage a reunion for Pat and her family at least every two years, either going to the U.K. or bringing Pat's parents to the U.S.

Unfortunately, we lost our wedding photo album in one of our many moves, so with the help of a few attendees who are still alive decades later, I have done my best to reconstruct the scenes as accurately as possible. What was never lost was the most important thing of all: the deep love Pat and I had for each other. Marriage was the ultimate touchstone.

It was the beginning of a new era—one that would bring countless moments of happiness. Pat and I would make our own family and do things together in a loving partnership. She was elegant, warm and intuitive with witty humor. She also made me feel like I could handle any responsibilities that came my way. I would try my best to meet her expectations.

# Chapter Fourteen

## Alexandria, Virginia

F ive months after the wedding, we packed our bags and set out for Washington, D.C. We were anxious to launch a new life, seek employment, find a home and start a family. In retrospect, our wedding might have seemed ordinary to others, but it was a grand wedding for us. Marrying Pat was the highlight of my life, a deep-rooted milestone of happiness. At that point, we belonged to each other in holy matrimony, obligated to offer our best effort in a bond of love.

We felt marriage was more than just a contract to stay together for the rest of our lives. It was a sacred bond. We now had the right to create and raise a family according to our values. Some may assume marriage magically gives them the right to control their spouse, but that was far from our belief. Marriage is a partnership and the ability to look past each other's mistakes, habits and work together. This ability strengthens with time, as does faith, trust, joint patience and endurance when thrust into the doldrums of hardships. We realized that not every relationship is perfect and there would be hurdles ahead, although we were two pieces in a puzzle that snugly fit together. We looked forward to our future, willing to face adversities in support of each other. This foundation made our marriage rock-solid, including faith, trust and other attributes.

We said our goodbyes in Port Arthur, packed our meager belongings in a U-Haul, hooked it up to the '54 Chevy and set out for D.C. As luck would have it, we got as far as Opelousas, Louisiana, when the transmission gave out. Luckily, my Uncle Joe Bono lived in Opelousas and we had a place to stay when the car was in the shop. We had a pleasant visit with Joe, his wife Raida and their family.

Bottom line, we spent most of our savings on a new transmission. We got rid of some of the items in the trailer to reduce the load and resumed our journey. When we arrived in the D.C. metroplex, it reminded me of a milestone when I was at MSG school five years earlier, poised to embark on a remarkable journey to London. Now, Jerry, Diane, Pat and I are meeting up again. We stayed with Jerry and Diane in their upscale townhouse in Alexandria, Virginia, until we rented an apartment.

We found the employment outlook was good during our job search and there was a wide selection of colleges to consider. Although, job hunting was not an easy feat, particularly when you rebound from one place to another for interviews in a crowded city. Back then, searching for a job was more time-consuming. But luck was on our side again.

Pat was first to find a job at a real estate firm in downtown D.C., which was not surprising. How could anyone resist hiring someone with such an optimistic outlook and a bubbly personality? Pat was not just a people-pleaser. She didn't have to do favors. It was the power of her nature that drew everyone towards her. She was able to relate to anyone and everyone.

Meanwhile, I continued my job search while Pat settled into her new job. Pat never showed disappointment when I had no job offers.

Instead, she was my source of encouragement, my counsel, boosting my spirit. Good fortune was on our side in terms of finances. Because Pat had a job and had a reliable income source, a benevolent banker loaned us money as a launchpad to settle in a modern, ground-floor apartment in Alexandria, Virginia. And enough money to purchase a set of slim-lined, Danish modern furniture on terms—fifty dollars down, twenty dollars a week. The furniture collection was ideal for apartment living and we were proud of the durable, easy to assemble, tongue and groove furniture. That style of furniture was perfect for us and lasted for several years.

We bought the furniture on a frosty Saturday morning at a store across town. Pat and I sat on the stylish oak parquet, bare wood floor, backs against a wall, waiting for the furniture to arrive. Obtaining furniture was another plateau as a couple. Perhaps most newlyweds feel the same way. Pat and I were ordinarily apathetic towards material 'things' per se, and furniture should've been just another thing. But neither of us contained our excitement.

As we waited in anticipation, Pat looked at her wristwatch and sighed. "They're over two hours late."

I scoffed. "Yep. Fast to take money, slow to deliver."

Pat peered out the sliding glass patio doors. A sheet of shimmering snowflakes floated from the sky, forming a white, transparent curtain across the landscape. A thick layer of snow blanketed the ground and poolside furnishings. It looked beautiful, but living through D.C. winters was a slow adjustment.

Pat said, "The snow is beautiful, but I'll be glad when we set up for a warm bed!"

I laughed. "It's supposed to get colder tonight," I said. "Remind you of home?"

Pat thought for a moment and nodded. "Yes, but I'm used to Texas weather now. It feels colder here!"

I said, "And it could ice over tonight, which means black muck on the roads and tire chains. I've never used tire chains before."

The furniture finally arrived. We were excited about making the apartment home, especially snuggling under warm blankets on a snowy cold Virginia night. But it didn't ice over that night as severely as I had predicted. The following day was somewhat cloudy, but the sun was shining. The wind felt fresh and chilly and it was pleasant, refreshing weather. The Virginia landscape was beautiful, especially when accented by the glittering snow. Everything was bright and appealing to the eye.

Pat went to work that Monday morning and I continued with my job search. One damp, cold, wintry day, I felt incredibly discouraged, more like gloomy. Being affected by the weather and seasonal changes is a loathsome condition. Besides allergies, instead of light, I see darkness. Being cooped up didn't help. I can hardly stand being constrained inside, in a bunker, whether self-imposed or not. The fact that I had no job yet added to the misery. I stood at the patio doors and watched the cloud over and sprinkle fluttering snowflakes. Melting snow began to form a thin layer of ice on the ground. Like a scene in the movie *Doctor Zhivago*, it was cold, gloomy, desolate—reflections of the winter of 1959 when I was in Marine Security Guard School a scant few miles away stuck in the barracks on weekends.

At that moment, I needed an emotional fix—a dose of Pat's uplifting optimism, her smiling face, her upbeat personality. I picked up the phone and called her.

After announcing the company name, Pat continued, "Can I help you?"

"Yes, you can help me—are you busy?"

"Oh, hi, Sweetie. I can talk."

With her classy Scottish inflections, her voice was spunky, cheerful. She was reliable and outstanding at her job, undoubtedly from a gifted species that made her an upbeat person. Over the years, I tried convincing her to become a professional broadcaster or actress in commercials. But she wasn't the ambitious type and was surprisingly shy about public speaking.

I said, "How's it going? Like your job?"

"It's great! The people here are nice, friendly and I like it a lot." She paused and lowered her voice. "How's it going for you?"

"Nothing yet."

"Don't worry. Something will come up. Soon."

She always encouraged me and an idea suddenly came to mind at that magical moment. Pat always had that remarkable effect on me.

I thought of a person in D.C. who could help—Congressman Jack Brooks from Beaumont, Texas. Brooks was also a Marine. The connection was a long shot, but it was worth a try. Brooks was a die-hard Leatherneck, a highly respected senior Congressman. He fought in WWII and retired as a full-bird Colonel. On his desk was a silver paperweight with the inscription *Fighting Marine*. Brooks served as a congressman for forty-two years, working under the speakership of fellow Texan Sam Rayburn.

"Sweetheart, I hate to cut it short, but I need to make a phone call."

My heart swelled with love for the woman who only had to say a few words of encouragement to boost my morale. No longer dreary, she renewed hope.

I immediately called Brook's office and left a message with his assistant. The next day, his office put me in touch with the hiring manager at the main post office in D.C. Within a week, I was unloading huge sacks of mail from box trucks down in the dungeons —the dock area. Ironically, it was reminiscent of a side job as a teen driver at the ambulance service. The ambulance service owner had a contract with the post office, making after midnight pickups at outlying substations and delivering to the main post office in Port Arthur. Back then my shift started at 11:00 pm, ending at about 7:00 am the next day. Fortunately, I had the company of DJs like J.P. Richardson (the Big Bopper) on KTRM radio in Beaumont. He played songs that kept the adrenaline going, easing the loneliness, keeping me alert. I inevitably packed the 24-foot box truck to the roof on the nightly pickup, making the truck top-heavy. Sometimes the truck dangerously swayed from side to side on windy nights. I hardly kept my eyes open one early morning, dozed off and caught myself veering into a ditch on Highway 69. I woke up just seconds before going into the ditch.

The D.C. postal job was unloading box trucks at the central station dock—a sweatshop at the busiest post office in the U.S. It was a tough job, but I was grateful for it. The downside was that working the night shift meant Pat and I rarely spent time together. Because of this, I went looking for another job.

After six months at the post office, I went to work for WTTG television in D.C. That's when I signed up for night classes in college. Going to school compounded an already tight schedule of late hours and fighting rush hour traffic. Up at 5 am, at work from 7:30 am to 5:00 pm and back home to wolf down a quick dinner. In those days, dollar pot pies were our staple diet. A treat was going out to dinner on paydays. Classes were from 6:30pm to 10:00pm. Afterward, it was homework into the wee hours, a few hours of sleep and it started all over again.

It wasn't like I was the only one who had it tough. Pat was also on a tight schedule, riding the bus to work downtown and she was always there to help me first. She was my cheerleader, a loyal partner who was there for me whatever the case. She looked at the brighter side of everything—citing the positives that most of us seem to miss. One might see bleak, dark skies and Pat would see sunlight and rainbows.

She also had some discouraging moments in her life. It was tough seeing someone so optimistic look gloomy and it occurred when she was pregnant with Peter. She came home sobbing one day after work, which surprised me. Pat rarely ever cried.

"Sweetie, what's the matter?" I asked.

I always felt a pang of pain when she cried. Maybe something happened at work. Perhaps she didn't have a good day, or she wasn't feeling well. A thousand thoughts ran through my mind per minute as I watched her sobbing heavily. Sniffling, she finally told me why she was crying.

"I rode on the bus standing all the way. No one offered a seat."

"I'm sorry. They probably didn't notice you were pregnant."

Having lived in London, I knew how courteous the Brits were to each other. Besides, Pat was a modest person. Except for nurturing an optimistic atmosphere, she was seldom demanding. For entertainment, we enjoyed inexpensive road trips in the country, picnics in the park and air shows at the local airport, where I underwent basic flight training. She fully supported my passions, even while creating a family, which required more significant finances.

Before long, various opportunities popped up, including lucrative government contracts. As a means to leapfrog financially, I gravitated to such opportunities.

# Chapter Fifteen

## Vietnam

In 1967, the Vietnam war was building steam and the government scrambled to hire former military people to operate in Vietnam. I worked in supply and logistics in the Marines and studied accounting in college, which qualified me for a job with an engineering firm. They had a contract with the U.S. Agency for International Development (USAID) to improve medical systems in Vietnamese hospitals. As a systems analyst, my job was to visit hospitals throughout southern Vietnam and recommend improvements in their medical supply chain. Pat and I carefully mulled over the trade-offs.

It was a matter of weighing financial opportunities versus threats. Did the danger of being hurt or killed outweigh the financial advantage? The upside was it would give us a giant leap forward financially. By this time, we had had our son Peter. Our primary goal was to invest in a house and build equity. And if I were to take the job, Pat and Peter could stay with Pat's parents in the U.K.—a delightful opportunity for Pat and her parents. My contract would only last 18 months, including vacation time to visit family in the U.K. Within that time frame, we could save enough money to buy a house and much more. Admittedly, a touch of adventurism influenced my thinking.

*Lou in Vietnam, between Nha Trang and Saigon, 1968*

When I left the Marine Corps, we were training for the war in Vietnam. But as a civilian "non-combatant," I would not travel to the front lines, the hot combat zones. Working in a war zone was not daunting; still, we would be working in the omnipresence of the National Liberation Front (Viet Cong or "VC"), the Vietnamese Communist guerilla forces. The VC operated in South Vietnam disguised as docile civilians during the day but were vicious fighters at night. Experts in covert jungle warfare, the VC adeptly conducted terrorism, ambushes and sabotage.

## Life in Wartime Vietnam

The highlight of a Saigon layover was reading Pat's mail, which I retrieved from the company office. Her letters were engaging, exciting, uplifting. She wrote about family gatherings, friends, the open market at Corby's town square and her general routine of raising the kids. Her letters intensified my yearning to be with my family. She had an attractive way of putting words on paper, describing things in an elegant, longhand manner. Pat's letters had been a treasure for me since before we were married when I was at Camp Pendleton and she was still in the U.K. When writing to her from 'Nam, I was cautious to keep my news mundane, sans dangerous situations. Of course, Pat knew there were no "safe zones" in Vietnam. Threats were everywhere, no matter the circumstances. One assignment turned out to be a rude awakening, a reminder that I was in a combat zone.

## Comforts from Home

After 12 months or so, I was ready to leave the Wild West environment of 'Nam and get back to my family. While still in the country, weekends off in Saigon were home base in some ways. A home away from home. I went to restaurants with Western-style menus and attended church on Sundays. The church was elegant, Saigon's beautiful Notre Dame Cathedral, built with French architectural influence. During worship services, I consistently thought about the significant missing part: Pat and Peter in England. After church, I would often go to an American-sponsored library and listen to recordings by the Beatles—the album "Sgt. Pepper's Lonely Hearts Club Band" was a favorite. A few years earlier, their song, "And I Love Her," had made me homesick, or more accurately, lovesick.

The Beatles' music—the British sensibilities—mystically enhanced Pat and Pete's remembrance in England, transposing me into that scenario with them. I savored my memories of the cottage, the pungent odor of a coal-burning fireplace, the double-decker buses and the town square market. My mouth watered for sausage-and-egg breakfasts and the sights of Corby. The church services, the Beatles' music, and fond memories of my fantasy world brought some sense of normalcy. I was lucky to have Pat and my family waiting for me, my liberators from the dregs of a screwed-up war. Thinking of family helped restore faith and civility. Pat was very faithful about writing letters, which were always uplifting and they intensified my yearning to be back together.

And then, at the point of thinking my work was "routine," the enemy launched the most significant attack in the war: the "Tet Offensive."

Tuesday, January 30, 1968, was a particularly sublime and welcomed day to start a holiday in Saigon. According to the lunar calendar, it was the New Year or "*Tet*" holiday in Vietnam. Tet is the Vietnamese celebration of rebirth, highly awaited and a source of fun and amusement. Things were quiet and laid back that day. That sense of peace turned out to be an illusion masking what was soon to come. That infamous night plunged into total mayhem that encompassed all of South Vietnam. It marked a historic military campaign, one of the biggest of the war.

While waiting for my next assignment in Saigon, I ran a few errands and lounged in my second-story apartment. I looked forward to watching the traditional Tet fireworks, colorful costumes and floats displayed by celebrants. I started the day writing and mailing a short letter to Pat, trying to stay in touch with life in the U.K. I didn't say much about the war, mainly focusing on work and each villages' local culture. Little did I know that on this fateful day, the danger would be right at my doorstep.

The night before the attack, I sat on a fold-up patio chair on my tiny balcony, enjoying the view below. The apartment building bore a striking resemblance to one in an iconic photo taken a few years later by a Dutchman, Hubert Van Es, showing refugees climbing a ladder to a helicopter atop an apartment building during the rescue of allies in Saigon. I propped my feet on the railing and peered down at the festive activity. A horde of Vietnamese chattered, chanted and whooped up the New Year celebration. Fireworks, costumes and fanfare lit up the night. Neighbors held festivities in a narrow alley-way, slowly progressing towards a crescendo at midnight. The celebration continued into the wee hours of the morning.

Then the unexpected "Tet Offensive" began with full force. Explosives shook the ground and lit up the sky with shattering effects. Ho Chi Minh's high-powered, formidable arsenal created everything from gunfire and artillery bursts to airborne flares and even massive rocket-generated fireballs. Amid the screams and mayhem, you could hear the menacing growl of engines and the clackety-clack of tracks crunching the streets—Soviet-made tanks. It was an all-out attack!

## Holed Up and Waiting

I dropped my feet to the floor and sprang from my chair. I rushed back into the apartment. Cell phones didn't exist then, and there were no landline phones in the building. I quickly switched the radio dial to Armed Forces Radio.

The announcement was to "Take cover. Stay in place until further notice."

The clatter of heavy equipment, small arms fire and rocket explosions created a collective echo of mass confusion on the streets below, where festivities had reigned just moments earlier. The NVA and Viet Cong had chosen the Tet holiday to launch the operation using coordinated surprise attacks on over 100 cities and outposts in South Vietnam. Under NVA's General Vo Nguyen command, an estimated 85,000 enemy troops pounced on designated targets in the early hours of January 31.

General Westmoreland, the U.S. forces commander, sequestered all U.S. civilians during the assault. I was alone in my studio apartment for more than a week until they imposed curfew hours. Luckily, I had an ample supply of food and drinks to last several weeks, the least of which were peanut butter, crackers, sardines and bottled water. I also had a Colt .38 Police Special and several boxes of hollow-point ammo. The six-round revolver wasn't necessarily an equalizer against the AK-47s wielded by the VC's Chu Luc (the main force), but it was much better than no weapon. If it were my time to go, I would take a few with me.

The enemy hit Tan Son Nhat airport heavily, which sadly injured several of my co-workers in the terminal. Daytime attacks were damaging, but nighttime activities were the worst. Fortunately, my apartment building, which housed several Americans, was a few miles from any significant military targets, so the bombings did not hit us. At bedtime, I tucked the fully loaded Colt under my pillow. Any sleep I got was minimal, with one eye cracked open, staring at the door. I had recurring nightmares of black pajama-clad VC soldiers charging through the door with beady killer eyes, holding hot firearms loaded for the kill. The added concern was not being able to notify Pat I was okay. I had no means of electronic communication, but the attack would be on the news worldwide.

The Tet brouhaha gave a new meaning to 'waking up in a cold sweat.' My body would be knotted stiff with anxiety, but I was physically and mentally alert. It could be a life-or-death situation—fear and adrenaline mandating fight or flight at any given moment. But the flight option was not doable.

# Chapter Sixteen

## Manassas to Bangkok

I t was a sacrifice to be apart, but the Vietnam assignment gave us a financial leap. I left Vietnam and reunited with Pat and Peter in England before the three of us returned to America. It was an exciting time, a fresh restart, a new beginning together. The stint in 'Nam resulted in a sizeable chunk of money to buy a house and more.

We went back to Virginia and bought a relatively new house in Manassas. Just off the famed interstate 66, Manassas is about 35 miles southeast of Washington, D.C. The town was a tiny, quaint bedroom community marked by clean air, little traffic and a laid-back atmosphere typical of small towns. The house was in a new project, with only a handful of friendly neighbors nearby.

I went to work for a small consulting firm in D.C. that developed and ran custom software for business clients. Headquartered in Wilmington, the company was a turnkey operation that competed directly with IBM's *Service Bureau*, the leading edge of business computing services at the time. Meanwhile, Pat stayed at home tending to Peter and later became pregnant with Angela.

Our house was a 5-bedroom, split-level, custom-built home with a fireplace upstairs and downstairs. Pat especially liked it because we had more than an acre lot, which set us apart from a few houses nearby. Beautiful Virginia Pine, Red Spruce and Eastern Red Cedar trees dotted the rolling hills. On the top side of the house, the large living room window framed a serenely scenic view of the multi-colored forestry. We enjoyed a superb sun deck off the breakfast area on the backside. On weekends, we sat on the sun deck, reading the newspaper and watching small airplanes fly overhead from the local airport, where I underwent my basic flight training. The place is now an expanded regional airport, hardly recognizable, no longer a "country" airport. While in basic training, flying above the Virginia landscape gave me a head rush. I reveled in its natural beauty. Pat and Peter hung out at the Manassas airport while training, but they preferred attending the annual air shows. The events were excellent for family gatherings, picnics and entertainment.

In town, Manassas's appealing amenities, such as an old-fashioned drugstore in the town square downtown, were full of nostalgic charm. It even contained a vintage soda fountain, complete with round swivel barstools. You'd think you had been transported back to the 50s, sipping a handmade cherry coke. The original small bottles of Coca-Cola wielded an illusion of the time I was a "soda jerk" at 9th Avenue Drug Store in Pear Ridge. The Manassas store also had vinyl-covered dining booths and an old-school café menu. We would often go there for a snack and a Coke while enjoying the traditional drug store environment.

In June 1969, Pat gave birth to our beautiful baby girl Angela at Prince William Hospital in Manassas. Angela's birth triggered my eagerness to advance my career to increase my income. At the same time, an opportunity came through some colleagues I had met in Vietnam. They asked me if I would want to set up a business in Bangkok, Thailand. They had already established a trading company in Saigon but wanted to startup a frozen beverage operation in Thailand. The idea appealed to the traveler in me. It was exotic enough to be exciting, but the people were friendly toward Americans. Plus, Western culture had filtered through enough to where Bangkok would have some of our established brands of food and supplies. Setting up the frozen beverage operation was sure to be challenging, but it also promised to be intriguing.

Pat and I discussed the pros and cons for a long time. We decided the second they offered acceptable terms. It was exciting, and for me, too adventurous to pass up. And it was agreed. We would go to Bangkok. We sold the house and right after that, IBM and Toshiba built a computer chip plant in Manassas. The plant would employ about 1200 people, which created a housing boom that, for better or worse, altered the quaintness of the town. Regardless, fond memories of Manassas and the Virginia countryside stayed with us.

The move to Bangkok was going surprisingly well. In a few weeks, we were on our way to distant places. Once again, Pat, Peter and Angela would stay with Pat's family in the U.K. It was an excellent opportunity for Pat to rejoin her family and it would be a special treat for Pat's parents—they hadn't even seen Angela yet, and were anxious to have grandchildren with them.

Pat's excursion to the U.K. was a significant positive. Despite the challenge of starting and running a business in a foreign country, visiting family in the U.K. swayed Pat's opinion. The plan was simple enough. I would fly straight to Bangkok to set up living quarters and an office, while Pat, Peter and Angela would fly to the U.K., stay with her parents, then join me later in Bangkok. After seeing them off at Dulles International Airport, I strutted to another airline to check in for a San Francisco flight.

I had a short layover in San Francisco, so I joined up with my cousin Marty—who was still in the Marines—and his fiancé' Judy. Those two troopers drove nearly 300 miles from Lompoc, Santa Barbara County. We had lunch together at Art's Café, a quaint, mom-and-pop diner that served delicious home-style eats. Sitting at the counter, you could peer into the kitchen and watch the cook's moves as he prepared the food—skillfully flipping burgers on the grill, mixing salads, multi-tasking. Martin and Judy bid me farewell at the San Francisco Airport and I was on my way to Bangkok.

Little did I know that in the future this airport would be the sight of a devastating occurrence.

## Bangkok

In the bustling city of Bangkok, Thailand, a six-foot concrete wall, topped with embedded glass shards, surrounded our 2,000-square-foot villa. And a wrought-iron gate extended across the driveway. Our compound sat a block from Sukhumvit Road, the main thoroughfare and a well-known street for shopping in Bangkok, a place of roughly 14 million people. Our backyard ended at a narrow, meandering canal—one of many waterways within Bangkok, the "Venice of the East."

One day after we had settled, Pat called me at my office and said, "There's a snake, . . . a *big* snake in the yard!"

The canal brought us an unexpected visitor that day—a gigantic King Cobra. Snake charmers use flare-winged Cobras, the longest venomous snakes in the world. I rushed home to find a Cobra in the yard, arched up with its flaps opened wide, staring as if to say, "This is my territory." It wasn't wavering, swaying side-to-side as they do for snake charmers. They oscillate because snake charmers burn incense to hypnotize them. It wasn't the case with this reptile. It stood majestically, non-wavering, tongue flicking, steely eyes fixed. I acted brave, unafraid of the creature in front of my family Generally not afraid of snakes, I felt a twinge of threat. Should I shoot it? Well, I didn't. One of our workers nonchalantly chased it away and all was calm. Growing up in Southeast Texas, you're accustomed to snakes and other creepy crawlers. We've had dangerous ones such as Water Moccasins in our yard, but the Cobra is a different breed, much more daunting. They can grow over 18 feet and weigh over 50 pounds. One day at the zoo in Bangkok, we watched a Cobra swallow a whole chicken just for breakfast.

On the matter of traffic, Sukhumvit Road was horrendous. Sizeable white buses and a multitude of vehicles used Sukhumvit Street daily. A usual scene was a horde of cars swarmed at a stoplight like bees on a honeycomb, trying to upstage one another. Often the jammed intersections were practically impassable. Then drivers would honk horns continuously, trying to maneuver and move in front. You need a horn, brakes and an accelerator to drive in Bangkok. Rules, road courtesy and common sense were practically nonexistent.

All in all, Bangkok had a variety of sights, sounds and smells—a charming place to tour, get to know the people and their culture. It was also a city with western-style food, stores and entertainment. Pat and I frequented "The Cave," a basement nightclub with live entertainment. One evening Pat requested the band play one of her favorite songs, "Sugar-Sugar" by the Archies. Surprisingly, they knew it, and the singer—a Filipino who sounded like Trini Lopez—sang it beautifully. True to form, Pat was full of energy and we danced most of the night through.

Our villa was in an upscale area of Bangkok and we assimilated with our surroundings quickly. As far as homemade food, a friendly neighbor—a retired Colonel from the Thai Army—gave us meals. He had a large compound on two acres adjacent to our place. Inside the compound was his main house and four other smaller homes. I think his entire family lived within the compound. They prepared meals from scratch, an all-day production, with various aromas drifting our way. I loved curry dishes and he would send us meals spiced with curry and peanut sauce. Clothed in casual "Ruean Ton" tube-style skirts, the Colonel's relatives assembled early in the day to chatter and prepared the ingredients. They used a mortar and pestle to grind and mash peanuts into a paste, mix in spices, then produce a sauce. Not sure what the ingredients were, but everything was fresh and the marinated meat was divine. I tasted traces of turmeric, ginger, cumin, chilis and of course, curry leaves. Pat hardly tolerated curry, but I savored it; when eating the spicy, delicate meals, my paranasal sinuses opened wide and cleared. My face oozed with sweat, but I enjoyed every minute of the cuisine.

For a better glimpse of Thai living conditions, consider provisional wooden houses on stilts along the banks of the Chao Phraya River, overhanging the water and paralleling the city's maze of canals (*khlongs*). Various rivers and tributaries that surrounded Bangkok fed khlongs. Khlongs are a significant part of Bangkok's transportation system—a waterway for small boats and gilded barges. The vessels travel up and down, passing scenes of busy people living on the banks, scrubbing clothes and doing household chores. Juxtapose Bangkok's waterway living with city living; you have a stark contrast with its modern buildings, a variety of fantastic restaurants, shopping malls and entertainment. In rural jungle areas, people are even more down-to-earth. Despite their earthy living conditions, they're very friendly and they smile a lot more than city folks. Doing the laundry means washing with buckets of rainwater. But there are also exotic beach resorts like the Patong Beach of Phuket, the largest island in Thailand.

The Thai culture reminded me of Vietnam, not too far away, on the other side of Laos. Thailand borders Laos to the east, Laos borders Vietnam, the coastline of the Gulf of Tonkin and the South China Sea. Bangkok sits at the southernmost edge, near the Gulf of Thailand. Laos's capital is Vientiane, about 400 miles north-northeast of Bangkok on the northern border.

During my time in Vietnam, I visited Vientiane, a hub base for Air America and the CIA. Surrounded by wartime activities, Vientiane was a haven for expatriate mercenaries—warriors huddled in a protected zone. Vientiane's outer perimeter was dangerous, but the town center was a haven for legionnaires from different countries. The only westernized nightclub suitable for foreigners was a zoo. Foreigners crammed the place like sardines in a can, like the amusing "Cantina Scene" in *Star Wars*. They were French, Australian, Spanish, Brits and other nationalities. Some wore makeshift uniforms. A solo singer—a Pilipino who sang like Trini Lopez—was scrunched in a corner. He only had a guitar, a mic and a rhythm amplifier box, but he sang *If I Had a Hammer* well, despite the dampening din of a crowd.

My previous experience in that part of the world helped us acclimate to Thailand's living conditions. There are different circumstances, but there is a common thread. They are of similar terrain, similar cuisine and lifestyle circumstances. And Bangkok had a mix of the same regimes but with modern, Western influence.

Family life in Bangkok was intriguing, a blend of local earthiness with access to new resources. We quickly adapted to their culture, but the main barrier was the language. Pat and I went to classes and learned enough Thai phrases to function in the Thai culture. We realized locals appreciate it when foreigners speak their language, even if not very fluent and blend with their lifestyles. The effort does matter to the locals. Shopping would become one of Pat's favorite hobbies while living there, especially bargaining with street vendors and she was good at it.

Shopping in Bangkok is a different beast. You can buy stuff at the Central mall stores and pay hefty prices or local markets where you pay low prices for fresh groceries. Even so, Thais treated foreign visitors well and appreciated our business. Pat thoroughly enjoyed dealing with local vendors. She was an expert at it. I can still visualize Pat squatting on her haunches haggling with a street vendor. Haggling is the preferred way of conducting business in that part of the world. The Thais would chuckle and smile, showing their reddened, betel nut-stained teeth. Like chewing tobacco and caffeine, betel nut is a stimulant, only much more potent. Supposedly, it triggers a feeling of euphoria. Maybe that's why the older folks smile so much.

At the markets, Pat was in her element. She bargained hard, face-to-face with local vendors. They loved it just as much as she did. If there were a standoff, Pat would shake her head and declare sharply, "Phaeng pai, phaeng pai!" *"Too expensive, too expensive!"*

Then she would get up with the theatrics of being done with it and strut away. After she had taken just a few steps, the vendors would call her back. Pat would slowly turn, walk around, squat again and resume the upper hand game. It was as good as any TV game show. The dealer would convert to Pat's terms, but once finalized, they would all have a hearty laugh together—a scene to behold and a reflection of her magic charm—a reminder of Pat's magnetic persona that attracted me the minute I first saw her. Likewise, the Thai people loved her down-to-earth attitude and willingness to blend with their culture. If you were unhappy or depressed, she would find the right words to lift you from the doldrums. Pat could brighten your day with empathy, her sense of understanding and passion and her quick wit. Her willingness and eagerness to adapt was a quality appreciated by many.

Pat was open to change and accepted change for what it was. Her optimistic outlook made the most of it. Pat had the right attitude to deal with different circumstances, recreate a compatible lifestyle, be happy. She typically saw an opportunity, not a problem. The one exception was having a maid come in to do house-cleaning and other chores. Her home was under her strict control and she took care of domestic duties. We lived in a compound, a pleasant and functional setup.

Pat, however, adamantly clung to her motherly household duties. Initially, it was challenging to convince Pat to have a maid clean the house. She eventually learned to accept the idea and appreciate the arrangement. We even had the use of a maid, but she was not a live-in. She was not a nanny per se, but that didn't matter. Her name was "Boonri," which meant "beautiful" in Thai. She had a baby with an American serviceman and loved the child immensely. Boonri incessantly played the song "I'm Not in Love" by the group "10cc." I suspect it was because she wasn't sure if she and the serviceman would marry, a common issue in Southeast Asia.

On a positive note, Bangkok offered a suitable schooling system for expatriates. I suppose it was because many foreigners were living there. We enrolled Peter in an international kindergarten school. Pat and I flipped a coin to decide who would take Peter to his first day at school. I was the one to do it and I'll never forget that day. It was more traumatic for me than for Pete.

As we drove off, I looked back and saw him staring at us with his dark brown eyes. It reminded me of the time at St. Pancras train station in London when he was four years old, looking up at me when I arrived for a visit from Vietnam. In Bangkok, looking at him standing there, my heart sunk; my eyes teared up. But his first day at school turned out well. When he came home from school, we asked him how it was. He liked it. He explained many types of students in his class, describing the differences in detail. He portrayed a class filled with different nationalities, skin colors and even a set of twins likely from Europe. At the time, Angela was too young for school. She was at home, where Pat and the staff were pampering her like a favorite doll.

The Thais loved Peter and Angela. They always cuddled them like loveable dolls. It made sense – white children were enough rarity to astound the Thais. They couldn't help but pick up Peter and Angela and hug them. And our maid was no exception. She sincerely loved them. Angela didn't mind since she was only a year old, but Peter didn't like being handled by strangers.

Anomalies aside, we assimilated well. Over time, we even adapted to eating food from push-cart street vendors. Thai food is almost dramatically different from our traditional food, but we developed a taste for it. The push-cart vendors would come by our compound daily and Pat would join our Thai employees to order food. Some favorite dishes included Pad Thai, stir-fried noodles and Wonton soup. We adjusted to local cuisine in time and we enjoyed dining at local restaurants.

As far as business, our first contract was a Catholic elementary school with hundreds of students. We set up a machine in a kiosk in the middle of the campus. It took a little time to ramp up, but we made a steady profit. We also set up a drink booth at the Asian Games in 1970. It was a big hit, with long lines of craving, thirsty customers. Frozen beverages were a perfect match in year-round temperatures between 82 to 86 degrees Fahrenheit.

The time we spent in Bangkok was pleasant and we learned a great deal about living and doing business in a foreign country. We also went on pleasure trips to places like Malaysia and Taiwan. We learned how flexibility, boldness and decisiveness are critical in an international environment. Even with all that, a partnership arrangement has risks. It's one thing to trust your friends outside the business context, but it's wholly different regarding money, decision-making and running a business. That's when conflicts are likely to arise and they did. The venture was so successful that others struggled to gain control. It was time to bow out; I had finished my part and we were ready to go back to the U.S.

Pat, Peter and Angela left in advance and went to stay with Pat's family in the U.K. and wait for me to join them later.

# Chapter Seventeen

## Pear Ridge, Texas

Going back to the U.K. was always exciting and a perfect transition point from Bangkok. Stopping over gave us time to spend time in Corby with Pat's family, get re-oriented to life in the western hemisphere. As enjoyable as it was to meet Pat's family it also gave us time to plan our trip back to the U.S., to start a new chapter. We went straight to Pear Ridge in Texas from England and temporarily stayed with my family until we settled.

Since I had left to join the Marines, Pear Ridge had mainly remained a rural community. When we moved there years ago, it had expansive pastures, but just a few blocks away from our house, a couple of grocery stores, a pharmacy and a service station on 9th Avenue. There was also a barbershop at 9th Avenue and 32nd Street called "Japs." I never figured out why they used that name. I don't recall ever going there because of its name. When I was a kid, the war with the Japanese burned a distinct correlation: "Japs" with "enemy." When I shared that with Pat, she thought that was the corniest thing she had heard. She laughed a long time over that. There were other "corny" things she heard about us youths in Port Arthur.

Pear Ridge was on the cusp of expansion and I'm glad Pat and the kids enjoyed the country-like environment before the buildup. I took Pat and the kids for a walk in the fields where we used to go bird hunting and fishing in what we thought were creeks, but in fact, were drainage ditches. Good thing we didn't eat what few fish we caught; no telling what was in that water.

Pat marveled at the story when we first moved to Pear Ridge. Dad, my brother Robert and I spent a whole day clearing the eastern pasture of waist-high growth. We used half-moon hand sickles and machetes and after a while, our arms felt like rubber. It was a hot summer day with the Texas sun bearing down and we were exhausted. With a sarcastic grin on his face, Dad peered over his gold, wire-rimmed glasses and said, "What's a matter? Can't keep up?"

He knew that would spur us on and it worked. He was a man of few words, and when he spoke, sort of like Pat, he wore a slight grin. Unless, of course, on a rare occasion when something would rile his Sicilian temperament, which was rare. Once, when I was a teenager, I was upset about something one day and said a curse word in front of Mom. Dad confronted me angrily, and we had a few words. That was a mistake on my part. The next thing I knew, the five-foot-two Sicilian had flipped me over and pinned my back to the floor. To this day, I don't know how he did it so quickly, so precisely at his age. I remember thinking for a short guy, he was tough as a bull. It was a lesson to remember. After that, I never said a foul word in front of Mom again. But the incident *was* an anomaly. We respected Mom and Dad, never used foul language, kept trouble away from them.

As I understand, it was the same with Pat and her family. The family was more focused on harmony, surviving together – getting a job, working, earning a living, and enjoying simple, social activities. I don't recall any conflicts in Pat's family. Pat and I were equally happy, having lived parallel lives through the '40s and '50s. We both came from hard-working, functional families. The depression had ended and most of us were in the same boat, as it was with Pat's family in the U.K. Britain was on the same path of surviving the global *Great Depression*, otherwise called the *Great Slump* in the '30s. The stock market crash in 1920 triggered the depression. Pat's parents talked about food rationing, registering at a store and obtaining a ration book to buy food. It was the same in the U.S. The government issued ration books for food, gasoline, tires and other short-supply items.

In those days of sacrifice, there was practically no peer pressure. Having fun was usually a simple affair and had nothing to do with drugs. Alcohol, yes, drugs, no. Fortunately, we had no interest in drugs during the '50s. We never heard the term "recreational drugs" until the '60s and even then, we had little interest in drug use, not even to try it.

In grade school, kids in my neighborhood used our half-acre lot next to the house to play sand-lot football and baseball. In our teen years, the pasture fell out of use. We were too busy chasing girls, playing organized sports in baseball and football. We fenced the field off and used it to keep a cow – our source for fresh, wholesome milk and delicious homemade butter. In time, the cow had a calf and between the two of them, they kept the grass down reasonably enough that I didn't have to mow the grass. Eventually, we sold the cow and calf and Dad cultivated the land for his garden. He drilled a well, rigged a submersible pump, and faithfully nurtured his garden with plenty of fertilizer, water and care. He didn't use insecticides, so the garden was strictly organic. Since the landscape is so close to sea level, Dad didn't go very deep to strike water. Water would likely spurt out like a gusher if you punched a four-foot hole in the ground.

He also built a chicken house and stocked it with a slew of chickens and chicks. We were never short of fresh eggs and chicken dinners. Best of all, they were organic and hormone-free. Watching Dad wring a chicken's neck and draining its blood was not a pleasant sight, but it meant a fried chicken meal was forthcoming. We sometimes had to help pluck the chicken but never clean and butcher it.

Various fruit trees dotted our yard, including a pomegranate, figs, pears and pecans. The cream of the crop was the fig tree that grew sweet, juicy, delicious figs the size of lemons. I used to pick figs straight from the tree and wolf them down until my belly swelled, not even bothering to wash the fruit before eating it. Few other fruits give instant energy and dietary fiber. Life in Pear Ridge was relatively quiet and straightforward, but the best part was how it accommodated self-sufficiency. In those days, we didn't have or need highfalutin' energy drinks. We gained energy from naturally nutritious foods straight out of Dad's Garden or the fruit trees in the yard. We had fresh milk from the cow, fresh vegetables, herbs, eggs, chicken meat, fruit and finally, Dad's homemade raisin wine.

Dad made raisin wine every year. His process never stopped being fascinating to me. First, he would reconstitute a batch of raisins by adding water. Then he would crush the plump raisins into a juice called "must." He'd pour the must into a vat, drop in some tablets, cover it with a towel and let it sit for a day. Then he'd add yeast and stir, using a wine press to cull out the skin and seeds. After that, he would pour the must into a 59-gallon, fire-seasoned oak barrel and add sugar. After stirring, it was ready for fermentation. He would insert a plastic tube through a hole in the cork down into the barrel and vent the carbon dioxide gas. The fermentation was the curious part of the entire process – I watched bubbles crawl through the tube, wondering how it was happening.

He kept the barrel in a cool dark spot in our barn. After several months, he would finally siphon off the translucent, residual liquid. The rest was consumable wine – brownish in color, on the fruity side, palate-friendly and very potent, as was evident on weekends. Every

Sunday, Dad washed down spaghetti dinner with a tumbler of wine and settled into his recliner chair. Minutes later, heavy snoring filled the room.

We usually had meat once a week on Sundays. Mom would sear a pork roast and boil it in the spaghetti sauce. On occasion, we had homemade Italian sausage as a side dish. Dad and Uncle Tony used to make the sausage when Tony stayed with us. I watched Uncle Tony grind the meat and stuff casing in the detached washhouse behind our house — a perfectly situated place for the operation since you couldn't smell the odors from inside the house. Adorned with strings of garlic and gourds from "Dad's Garden," the washhouse also contained a well-used, vintage 1950s wringer-washing machine.

Sometimes Mom would make pasta by hand. Usually, egg pasta hung in the kitchen like doughy string curtains to dry. You had to duck and dodge your way through the kitchen then, or you ran the risk of a pasta tassel slapping you in the face or flicking you in the eye. It was hard enough getting through the kitchen.

We stopped using water from the well and tapped into city water lines. The old water well had a cylindrical concrete base with a raised roof, a hand wheel and a water bucket. It was ornate, but we eventually plugged it and removed the structure. The city water was more convenient.

We did the same with the wood fireplace. We sealed it off but left the chimney, the frame and the mantle in place. Fronting the hearth was an old-style gas heater. On cold, damp winter mornings, the space heater was the center of many a sibling conflict. We huddled around it, trying desperately to repress the frosty air that seeped through the floor from under the house and chilled the marrow in our bones. Most homes in Southeast Texas had gas space heaters. Central heating and air were a luxury. We had gas space heaters and attic fans. Putting in our first window air conditioning unit was an arduous milestone that I remember well. It was a hot, sweltering day when I had to snake my way under the house in slimy black-gumbo mud to install the wiring. Our house had initially been a duplex farmhouse constructed in the late 30s. Electrical wiring was often shoddy.

To connect the two sections of the house, Uncle Gene installed doors in the partition. He effectively converted the house into a three-bedroom home fit for a single-family, complete with a shared bathroom and kitchen area. Presumably, there had been an outhouse when they built the house. In time, the bathroom became part of the back-porch addition. Regardless, the house was relatively small for seven to eight people.

To save money on the water bill, Dad put in another well next to his garden to feed the plants. He grew a mix of vegetables, including Cannellini beans, garlic, Sicilian hot peppers and several herbs. Sicilians are inherently farmers. Dad's Garden invariably produced the biggest, juiciest vegetables I've seen. The garden was his work of art, a mosaic that he nursed daily. He worked the soil with bare hands, weeding, watering and protecting it from pests.

Visions of Dad and his garden are priceless. A common sight was Dad standing at the edge of his garden, scanning it through his round, metal-rimmed glasses. He stood with his shirt sleeves rolled to his elbows and hands on his hips. Dad would proudly pan his garden for several minutes at a time as if encouraging it to grow. He usually wore khaki trousers with a chain attached to a belt loop. This chain linked to a gold watch nestled in a small watch pocket. He would routinely pull out the worn, shiny watch — inscribed with *"38 years"* given to him by the Texas Company — and check the time. His routine was getting up early, going to work, coming home, tending to his garden, checking the time and doing chores.

Dad lived for 86 years until he stopped working and became ill. Undoubtedly, his genes and a lifestyle combining work, garden, laughter and wine contributed to his long life. Mom's genes and life-style furthered a life of 88 years. Her work, belief in God, and dedication were the foremost tenets of her life. Mom and Dad were icons of an exceptional generation and we miss them dearly.

# Chapter Eighteen

## Dallas, Texas

After returning from Bangkok in 1973, we stayed with my family in Pear Ridge for three months. During the transition, I went to work for a banking consulting firm based in Dallas. My first assignment was at the Republic National Bank in downtown Dallas and I became a bona fide "road warrior." I flew out of Jefferson County Airport every Sunday directly to Dallas and returned on Friday. I stayed in a hotel five days a week for eight weeks.

Dallas was rapidly growing and offered many opportunities. Meanwhile, Pat and I pondered where we would resettle.

"Where would you like to live? I asked Pat. "Back in Virginia?"

"Not sure yet. What about your job here?"

"It doesn't matter where we live. If I'm close to an airport able to fly to job sites, it's okay."

She paused. "I like it here in Texas. The people are friendly."

"How about Dallas? Looks pretty good to me."

"Okay."

I gave a thumbs up. "Dallas, here we come."

It was the right decision. Dallas was a clean city, an attractive place to raise a family. It showed signs of a healthy economy, with excellent school systems and many job opportunities, so the area appeared perfect for us. Pat and the kids enjoyed living in Port Arthur, but staying there wasn't feasible in terms of a career. It hadn't changed much from when I left in 1958. It was essentially a one-industry town with few prospects for pursuing my career goals. Ambition drove me to turn away from a slow-moving routine. The good jobs were at the refineries, which was not my bailiwick.

One chilly weekend in November, we packed lunches and gassed up our 1964 metallic emerald-green Cadillac sedan, a car we bought from my cousin Johnny Tatman. Peter and Angela crawled into the back seat and we headed to Dallas. The Caddy was like a luxury cruise ship, big and roomy. The car sailed smoothly over the highway with its superior suspension, aerodynamic design and groovy shark fins on the tail end. The ride was so smooth that Peter and Angela slept on the king-size back seat most of the way. After a brief tour of Dallas, it didn't take us long to finalize our decision to move there. Our first place in Dallas was an apartment in a conclave tucked between LBJ Freeway and Highway I-45. It was a new apartment complex in a nice neighborhood and there were kids the same age as Peter and Angela.

In short order, Pat went to work as secretary to a local bank president during the day and part-time receptionist at a Marriott hotel in the evening. As long as it didn't interfere with family life, she was a glutton for work, an inherited trait. Pat was an exemplary employee in every job situation of her life. Before Peter's birth, she worked for two years at J. Frank Phillips real estate firm in Washington, D.C. After we moved to Dallas, she worked for four years at J.J. Pierce High School in Richardson, which allowed her to be at home when

Peter and Angela were home from school. Then she served a seven-year tenure with the Bent Tree National Bank in Dallas as Executive Assistant to the President and a customer service representative. After that, Pat spent five years with Rector Properties, a commercial real estate firm. In between jobs, she also worked part-time for Marriott-Radisson in Dallas. She had a penchant for not only being a super mom but a reliable, hard worker in the commercial world.


## Moving Up in the Computer World

Meanwhile, the computing industry was on the upswing, growing leaps and bounds. I accepted a sales rep job with the University Computing Company (UCC). Savvy entrepreneurs Sam Wiley and his brother Charles started the company in 1963 with only $1,000 and a business idea: lease time on a university's system and using their computers, resell services to business clients—hence the name, UCC. Sam secured contracts with Texas Instruments, Sun Oil Company and Southern Methodist University in Dallas. In those days, as a sales rep, you hit the road with a roll of dimes and calling cards to visit prospects. There were no cell phones then, so we used payphones in the field. Electronic contact and selling over the phone were not practical in the industry—we set up meetings in the area, wearing a suit or at least a dress shirt and tie. We had email, but many didn't. We used an embryonic command-line form of email in the late 60s-70s. At that time, mainly government contractors used the system to coordinate projects. UCC chalked up $57 million in sales in a short span of five years and became a premier company.

After leaving UCC in 1969, I went to work for another embryonic company, Storage Technology Corporation ("STC," now called StorageTek, or "STK"). Founded by Jesse Aweida and three co-founders who were former IBM engineers, the company designed and developed tape backup drives in competition with IBM equipment. We were outnumbered ten to one by IBM's formidable marketing force.

But STC is another success story. The company grew to become highly successful and I am proud to have been a small part of it. Besides Texas Instruments, one of my key accounts was legendary Ross Perot's Electronic Data Systems ("EDS"). Perot, a former IBM employee, started EDS in 1962 with a small investment and a contract to process medical claims for Blue Cross-Blue Shield. From there, Perot and his company blossomed into a huge success.

Working with innovative, successful companies inspired me to start a computer firm, Mana-Tech Company, in 1978. We designed and developed turnkey business systems for multiple industries, including mini-computers, software, follow-on support and online database management. For a while, Pat worked with me in this endeavor. We eventually sold the company and I went into independent IT consulting work.

While consulting for several companies—Raymond James and Verizon, to name a few—I invested in a new Dallas venture, AsiaInfo Services, Inc., in the early 90s. Chinese nationals partially owned the company, working under U.S. visas and full citizenship. We followed the news feed from China, and one of my roles was Executive Editor of a Chinese online news service. We received a compilation of 50 summarized articles from China daily and I rewrote them for electronic distribution via Forbes, Bloomberg, Fortune, Wall Street Journal and others. The beginning of a new era incorporated the Internet's power in international commerce, particularly in China's economic buildup.

This historic project implemented the first commercial Internet connection in China. The Chinese only had a minuscule Internet system among education institutions at that time. We implemented "ChinaNet," a network designed for universal use, working with Sprint Corporation. The first two nodes were Beijing and Shanghai, beginning China's commercial connections and their enormous internet surge. We used to call it "The Information Highway." Our company hosted numerous Chinese trade delegations visiting Dallas. I often escorted top officials from communications ministries in China, dined with them, and rubbed shoulders as they became acquainted with our lifestyle and values. Our project was an essential ingredient for international economic growth between China and the U.S. For that matter, we equipped China with a cyber pathway for commercial development across the globe. As it turns out, China and other nations have weaponized the Internet.

Today, I cringe to think I played a role—albeit a small one—in a strategic plan, a movement to advance the Chinese Communist Party's aggressive agenda against the U.S. and the world. We paved the way for establishing a formidable tool in China—the Internet. We conducted training classes for Chinese IT operators at Sprint headquarters in Reston, Virginia, as we installed the infrastructure. Sprint International was part of the contract project. I should have known what the future would bring when the Chinese rigged the Internet software for political censorship and spying.

When I learned they had embedded filtering software to detect and call out political dissidents who could end up in "reeducation camps," it was a bellwether moment for me. Another was when we wrongly decoupled China's human rights issue from trade policies. Now, the Chinese use the network I worked on for nefarious purposes, such as cyber warfare, espionage, human abuse and political corruption. In collusion with world oligarchs, China has penetrated the network of political hacks with influence, which poses an extreme danger to world peace as evidenced by current affairs. For me, it is a traumatic wave of sickening repulsion.

## Accomplished Offspring, Proud Papa

After renting an apartment for a year, Pat and I bought a modest house in North Dallas with three bedrooms, two bathrooms, a small kitchen, a living room, a dining room and a 2-car garage. The house was in a quaint middle-class neighborhood near strip malls, schools and easy access to freeways. Our neighbors had children the same ages as Peter and Angela, and we were two blocks from an elementary and junior high school. We used to barricade our street and have block parties. It was enjoyable to develop a circle of friends, particularly in sports and music, the interests our children pursued. Angela got into sports. Peter was also a good athlete, a fast runner on the soccer team, but more interested in music. Pat and I often went in different directions, either to a soccer game, track meets, volleyball game, or a school concert where Peter played the saxophone. Why the sax? I believe a series of events led to this decision.

One day Peter came home from elementary school and told Pat, "I want to join the band."

"Really? So, what instrument would you like to play?" asked Pat.

Pete thought for a moment. "I'm not sure."

"How about the saxophone?"

"Okay, I'll give it a try."

When he was ten years old, I took him to see Boots Randolph (of *Yakety Sax* fame) at a dinner theater. Peter fixed his eyes on Boots the entire evening without missing a beat. Peter has played the saxophone, other wind instruments and the drums from that point on. He played in the school band through junior high and high school and took private lessons. One day we received a call from his instructor, who said, "You need to get a better saxophone for Pete. The rental horn is not doing him justice, especially in jazz."

The next day, I told Peter, "Your instructor said you need a better saxophone. Now, if we buy you a better horn, you'll have to make it pay off."

Peter smiled. "Thanks, I'll do my best. I like jazz."

He achieved a most exceptional music award in his senior year of high school—the All-State Band. Peter went to Knoxville, Tennessee, for the Music Educators Association's All-State Jazz Festival; Pat, Angela and I packed our bags and followed him there, stopping along the way at tourist hot spots. That was a delightful trip—one of those jewels in the box—the All-State band and the All-State Jazz Festival.

Peter is still a dyed-in-the-wool musician and the investment in his lessons and that new sax has paid off many times over. He was soon placed directly into that school's revered One-O'clock Lab Band—the first transfer student to chair in the lead band. On a music scholarship, Peter attended the University of Miami and later played in "ghost bands" like those begun by Woody Herman, Glenn Miller, Stan Getz, Artie Shaw, Tommy Dorsey and Maynard Ferguson to name a few.

Pete has accompanied countless other stars and icons in classic pop, dance-band and jazz fields. He's been on international tours with several big bands, notably one event I attended in England after my trip to Sicily and the U.K. in 2001 when Peter was on tour with the Woody Herman band. Pat's sister and her husband, Jackie and John McInulty, were there. The venue was a dance hall in a town outside Leicester, England and the Woody band backed Frank Sinatra, Jr., who is much like his father and a very unpretentious, friendly person. On another tour, Peter also played at Ronnie Scott's club in London. The place Pat and I frequented years before.

In Angela's case, she showed athletic abilities and a strong sense of self-defense. She had lots of self-confidence even as a child. One day when she was in the fifth grade, I looked out the front window and saw two boys hassling her on our front lawn. Suddenly, she flipped one of them down to the ground, straddled him and pinned his arms back. The other kid's eyes bulged with fear and he quickly backed off. The situation was well under control—no need for Dad's help—and she's been that way ever since, fending for herself and helping others.

Another time, a couple of her friends were fist-fighting. Angela stepped in to stop them and she came home with a black eye. Of course, it was an accident, but it stopped the fighting!

Angela's natural agility, speed, endurance and competitiveness put her in many sports at school—volleyball, basketball, softball, track and soccer. She excelled, especially in track, in which she participated in private clubs during summer months. We endured long trips to attend lengthy track meets in the scorching heat. Angela won the regional race in the Jesse Owens tournament and went to Los Angeles to run in the national competition. She undoubtedly inherited speed from Pat and her dad Albert. Down the line, if there ever were a natural athlete, that would be our grandson, Gavin. He inherited the innate athletic abilities of both Angela and her husband, Ronnie.

When Angela was eleven years old, she joined the internationally recognized championship "Sting" soccer club in Dallas—the youngest player recruited. The club notably won many titles over the years. At least one of the players went on to play for Team U.S.A. Angela continued to play in her adult years in various leagues in Dallas. One rare incident occurred when the referee ejected her during an indoor soccer game in a co-ed league. Angela played forward, and one of the guys, a fullback, was continually roughing Angela, body-checking her. Like in a hockey game, he threw his body into her, elbowing and knocking her against the sidewall. Angela got fed up and started shoving back, poking her elbow in the guy's ribs. Of course, the referee saw Angela retaliate but did not see the other player's initial infraction. He blew his whistle, red-carded Angela and she was out of the game. According to the rules, the referee wasn't supposed to penalize women in that league, only the men. Chalk up another first for Angela. Pat chuckled and I stretched a proud, broad smile across my face. Angela's coach complained but wasn't surprised Angela retaliated.

After Angela waived soccer scholarship offers from other colleges, she attended the University of North Texas in Denton, Texas. Angela played amateur adult soccer until she had injuries to both knees. After having ACL surgery on both knees, she eventually hung up her cleats and concentrated on her real estate business. Following Pat's lead, Angela was interested in real estate early on. As a child, she often accompanied Pat to tour open houses for sale, a hobby of Pat's. When Angela was about eleven years old, Pat asked her, "What do you want to do when you grow up?"

"Sell houses."

After graduation, she earned her license and is now a very successful agent in the Dallas area. Working for top firms in Dallas, Angela has won many awards in the industry. She received the 2018 Top Individual Agent for Total Units Closed and Top Gross Commission Income in her office.

Undoubtedly, Peter and Angela inherited much of their natural abilities from Pat. Pat may not have been ambitious in business to rise to executive levels, but she was top-notch in what she did. She was a people person, a stellar singer, dancer, athlete, a wonderful, loving wife and mother.

While in Dallas, soccer was a big part of our family life. In addition to coaching youth soccer, Pat and I played adult soccer. Our club included Pat's team, the Tuff Muthas and four men's teams. Our players ranged from semi-pro level to beer-gut, over-the-hill guys— where I eventually ended up. We co-founded and managed the club for about five years, and I think I was in the best physical shape since my military days. Pat was also in good physical condition, except for a few bouts of hyperventilation. We always had a brown paper bag for Pat to breathe, to recirculate carbon dioxide back into her lungs. In the days before soccer became pervasive in Dallas, a group of us organized the "Hotspurs" club. Our logo was a soccer ball with horse spurs gripped around it on the boot's heel. The name mimics the official English soccer team, the *Tottenham Hotspurs*. While on duty in London, I had often walked from the train station to visit Pat in Islington; on the way, I would pause to watch the Hotspurs—a favored team—practice in a nearby field.

*Pat at Tuff Muthuhs Soccer Game – Dallas, 1983*

During those days in Dallas, our lives revolved around the soccer crowd, a group of fun-loving friends that believed in playing hard and partying hard. We all had responsibilities, jobs, mortgages and kids about the same age, so the boozing wasn't that wild—just the usual drill for parents on weekends. Our group was very engaged, active, socially compatible and responsible, but we also loved to celebrate.

## Sky's the Limit

Besides working and enjoying family life, I took the time to complete my commercial instrument flight training at Addison Airport. Then I continued at Dallas Love Field for multi-engine jet training. After receiving my instrument rating, I began training in an eight-passenger

Model 501 Cessna Citation I, the first Cessna bizjets model. At that time, it was the only Citation rated for single-pilot capability. The bird was a different feel compared to a prop-driven plane. It had more instruments and procedures to keep up with and the need to think ahead of such a fast-moving plane.

The sleek plane belonged to Enrico Cortez (an alias), a wealthy business owner in Monterrey, Mexico. The bizjet was part of about six airplanes based in Monterey. My flight instructor, Hank Moseley and I often flew out of Dallas's Love Field Airport to Monterrey to shuttle Cortez's family back and forth to colleges in the U.S. and Cortez's business meetings.

Love Field was our base, but Cortez's home base was a private airport nestled in Monterey's surrounding mountains. A cadre of wealthy Mexicans, including Cortez, purchased what used to be the regional airport until they built Monterey International Airport nearby. Fleets of airplanes owned by the group occupied the airfield.

We took off from Dallas in the early morning hours. I was the PIC—pilot-in-command—and Hank was in the right seat as co-pilot and instructor. On my approach to Monterrey, I flew over the mountains and descended into the "soup bowl," the valley between mountains where Monterrey, much like Los Angeles, sits in a plume of pollution. Hank pointed to the small, uncontrolled airstrip and said, "At your ten o'clock."

I scanned the landscape to no avail. "Can't see it. Where is it?"

He pointed again and said, "There, near that group of buildings."

I finally spotted a thin, obscure Band-Aid of a strip. I was expecting a much larger runway, but this one was like a country runway. I assessed the landing conditions. There was no wiggle room, no room for error. *Man, this could get tricky—surrounding mountains, crosswinds and a short, narrow runway to plant this bird.*

Fences lined both sides of the tiny airfield, so maneuvering a twin-engine jet to a touchdown groove was like threading a needle. Due to unpredictable winds, the slightest deviation in my landing could push me off centerline or cause me to overshoot or fall short—there wasn't much room for error. Particularly when you land at a strange airport, you have to assess your situation, not fret, but assess. Aside from a few minor control adjustments, I landed the Citation just fine. It was challenging but fun!

After touchdown and rollout, Hank said, "Well done for your first time here." Then he pointed to a rustic hangar. "Park it there."

We had a two-day layover in Monterey—enough time to become acquainted with Cortez's bodyguard team. As affluent as he was, Cortez needed protection. Wealthy Mexican families are targets for kidnappings, a specialized income source for drug cartels and organized crime networks.

Cortez, Hank, the cluster of bodyguards and I all went to dinner that first night. Hank sat with Cortez and his associates while I had the privilege—I thought—of sitting at the table with the husky, intense bodyguards with weapons. I wanna call them Cortez's "Goon Squad," but that would be inaccurate and disrespectful. They were capable professionals, not as polished as the Secret Service, but daunting and fearsome tough guys. They passionately fulfilled their job and contractual duties.

However, being sociable was not a requirement or part of the bodyguards' mission. None of them made eye contact, smiled, or spoke with me all evening. I felt an aura of danger and uneasiness among these guys while in a foreign country. I was without a weapon and bulletproof protection, and criminals targeted Cortez as a kidnapping opportunity. The scenario was reminiscent of Vietnam, not knowing who or where the enemy was and when things would happen, but ready to hit the deck in case of incoming explosives, firepower, or a suicide bomber riding towards you on a bike.

What's worse, the Mexican food I was eating was an earthy-smelling pork dish with a rancid taste. The food and the dangerous atmosphere made my stomach feel swollen and nauseous. My head pulsated with every heartbeat. The fear of food poisoning gripped me, so I headed back to my hotel room. The smug-faced bodyguards nodded to acknowledge my departure. I downed a few swigs of *Pepto-Bismol* in my hotel room, took some aspirin and chased it with some *Carta Blanca* beer. For the moment, that did the trick. I'll skip the ugly details.

I finished my preflight checklist the following day and sat in the cockpit, waiting for Cortez's entourage. Five cars drove up to the airplane. It was like a scene in a James Bond movie, only in natural living color. I looked down into the two lead cars and spotted AK-47 and AR15 rifles next to the stone-faced bodyguards on the front seats. They also had 10-millimeter Glock pistols in shoulder holsters. After everyone had boarded, Cortez's family of two sons and a daughter. We fired up the Pratt & Whitney engines, taxied toward the runway and took off in the misty mid-morning air. I was again the PIC and Hank was the co-pilot. *Hot-dog, I'm flying as a commercial pilot.*

After lift-off and going through the checklist, I angled my head to scan the instruments while maneuvering to my course heading. *Everything looks good. No turbulence, all set.* Then Hank took the wind out of my sails. He leaned over, cupped his hand to his mouth and whispered, "Look up, straight ahead." I lifted my head and looked out the windscreen. A colossal mountain loomed ominously in front of us. It was miles away, but I quickly altered the course a few degrees and added more throttle. *Doggonit. I was doing so well.*

Hank leaned over and whispered again, "Had your head in the cockpit."

In other words, I was focused on the instrument panel for far too long and not the terrain. Too long was a matter of seconds. As Cortez's chief pilot, Hank spent a lot of time in Mexico and probably did a lot of carousing. Some months later, I received the sad news that he'd been shot and killed by someone in some dispute involving a man and a woman at a cantina in Monterey. I was stunned. Hank was a good guy, but mingling with women in Mexico was a bad habit. He had a heart, was easy to get along with and was one heck of a flight instructor. He used to buy gifts handcrafted in Mexico for Pat and me. Trinkets like brass airplanes, motorcycles and ceramic figurines. Today, a couple of these items are still on my bookcase—memorabilia from the past, fodder for reflection.

## Auld Acquaintance Celebrations

By the late 80s, we had lived in the North Dallas-Richardson area for nearly twenty years. With such a great group of friends, we stopped going to public places for New Year celebrations and elected to hold a party at our house. It was a big hit; it became an annual practice, a tradition that our entire group of friends eagerly anticipated. The crowd grew bigger and bigger. After a few years, our three-bedroom house could barely hold a shoulder-to-shoulder bunch, so we converted the garage into a den. Even when the weather was terrible, a modest crowd would show up. Once when we had an ice storm, power lines were down and we were without electricity. Still, about two dozen people came to the house. We burned wood from an old fence I had torn down for heat and we used a battery-operated radio for music.

Some guys even competed for being the last one to leave. When I was ready to shut down the party, I would point to the couches and say, "There are your beds," then point down the hall and say, "Mine's back there and don't wake me up!"

The mornings after were unforgettable. Our house had the stench of a bar. Typically, the guys on the couches were still there. My brother Robert and I would head for downtown Dallas to an Italian grocery store to buy fresh Italian sausage and "Cucidati" fig cookies (after Peter and Angela opted out of helping me make sausage and fig cookies). We would fix a traditional breakfast at the house, including Italian sausage, for good luck. We sometimes included the time-honored Americana-style black-eyed peas.

Undoubtedly, the success of the New Year's party was because of Pat. She was the primary influence for a festive, joyful atmosphere. I handled the music and she used her innate talent to inspire people and create a happy, vibrant atmosphere like a Scottish gathering. She instituted a custom: when the clock struck midnight, everyone would stream out to the front yard and holding hands, form a moving circle singing the traditional New Year's song from her native Scotland, "*Auld Lang Syne*." It was a unique, beautiful, memorable tradition that many of us cherished—and still do.

# Chapter Nineteen

## Light to Darkness

Fast forward to the year 2000. As a contractor, I traveled out of state. It was a good year despite being miles apart—until it wasn't. When I was in California working under contract, we spent quality time together during the summer months. We did touristy stuff in Northern California and Pat thoroughly enjoyed the time off from her job in Dallas. The extraordinary scenes of San Francisco dazzled her. She marveled at the steep hills overlooking the bay, the Golden Gate Bridge and the historic architecture of San Francisco. She loved the thrill of riding the iconic cable cars, walking through Chinatown and stopping for a taste of Dim Sum, a popular Chinese breakfast snack. We visited Ghirardelli Square toured the chocolate maker's factory and other landmark sites such as Union Square, Little Italy and Nob Hill. San Francisco was thrilling and quaint, with a host of excellent restaurants and tons of unique charm.

By coincidence, Pat's cousin Michael lived in San Francisco. He had moved from Scotland to the U.S. via Canada. Michael lived on Lombard Street—a beautiful, bougainvillea- bedecked meandering thoroughfare sometimes referred to as "the most crooked street in the world." It is well-manicured and a popular tourist attraction. It winds through the lovely upscale Russian Hill district, with its beautiful flower gardens accenting magnificent Victorian-style mansions.

One evening, we visited Michael at his house. Then we went to an exclusive restaurant where he treated us to a fantastic steak dinner complemented by fine Sonoma Valley wine. We thoroughly enjoyed the evening, discussing former times in Scotland and how---- Michael ended up in San Francisco. He was about eleven years old the last time I'd seen him.

Michael was one of Pat's cousins who played American football with me in Aberdeen. Conversation flowed smoothly that evening over dinner. It was a joyous reunion, a recollection of days together in Scotland. We reminisced about another evening years earlier, a visit to a pub in Aberdeen with Michael, Pat's dad and several other relatives, including her uncle Beatty, a baker with a very heavy brogue—sometimes I could hardly understand him. He made mouth-watering bread and pastries in his bakery downtown.

## Mineola and Emeryville

As we were catching up with each other over dinner in San Francisco, the conversation turned to life in Dallas and the lake house we had purchased in Mineola, Texas. The small town of Mineola is a little over 80 miles east of Dallas a straight shot on highway 80. Mineola is a quaint town with a pleasant country atmosphere. Our house was on the bank of Lake Holbrook, a small-scale private lake, free of weekend rowdies. It was a getaway place for us, though we didn't spend much time on the lake; we enjoyed going there but mainly worked to take care of the property. The area had a couple of small airports, one of which—Wiesner Field—had a fleet of vintage Boeing Stearman Model 75 biplanes, which I piloted a few times with help from an instructor. The quaint airport was one of our hangouts, as it was for several retired airline pilots living in the area. Even after we sold our lake house, we continued to visit Mineola, eat brunch at a rustic restaurant and make the rounds.

On one occasion, when we went to Mineola, Mom was with us. After we parked at the restaurant and got out of the car, I said, "Stop. Listen." Pat and Mom stopped with ears perked. Pat paused, then said, "I don't hear anything. Maybe a bird chirping."

"That's the point. You hear mother nature."

Occasionally, when I called Pat from Emeryville on weekends, she would be in the car on her way to Mineola like we did before. It was a simple way of relaxation, presumably in remembrance of our times there together at the country restaurant.

That same year in 2000, while in California, we explored the Bay Area with Pat's sister Jackie and her husband John, visiting from England. I had to work that day, but they toured Fisherman's Wharf and Alcatraz, the former federal prison on an island a mile or so offshore in the bay near San Francisco. In the past, the isolated prison had been home to infamous gangsters such as George "Machine Gun" Kelly, Al Capone and Robert Stroud, "The Birdman of Alcatraz." According to local folklore, the place is haunted, but Pat, Jackie and John thoroughly enjoyed the tour. Upon their return to Fisherman's Wharf, they stopped at one of several restaurants serving delicious clam chowder and sweet, tender Dungeness crab. It was great having them visit the Bay Area.

After Jackie and John resumed their journey back to England, Pat continued her stay in Emeryville, reading books on the pier and enjoying free time. Meeting up with her sister and her husband was a special treat; we had not seen them for several years. The vacation was a bright light of happiness for Pat.

When she left California for Dallas, everything was normal. But her next visit months later was the beginning of the darkest, most disturbing time Pat and I had ever experienced.

## Flying in the Dark

In November 2000, Pat had another stay in Emeryville, albeit a more laid-back one. After her two-week visit, it was time for her to return to Dallas. We were in the airport terminal when Pat's shining light faded, and the worst was yet to come.

The horrible experience at San Francisco Airport—the account I began this book with— was the genesis of my gut-wrenching nightmare, one that re-emerges in remnants that are as traumatic and haunting as they were then. The episode brought on the same unanswerable question: why should someone as giving and loving as Pat suffer when others, seemingly less deserving, sail through a long life unscathed?

After tearful Pat entered the dark tunnel and boarded the airliner, I couldn't get to her, triggering an internal alarm. After wrangling with the airport security guards, I spun around and jogged through the airport to the parking garage, then whizzed down the parking ramp, paid at the kiosk and made a quick exit to the freeway. Racing back to the apartment, speeding, weaving through traffic, I could've easily wrecked the car and killed myself. At one point, I pegged 90 miles per hour on the freeway. When I arrived in Emeryville, I booked the first flight to Dallas, threw a few things in a travel bag and rushed back to the airport.

Before leaving the apartment, I had called Pat on her cell phone. Luckily, her flight had a layover in Las Vegas. Thank God, she answered. It was a tremendous relief to hear her voice.

I said, "Sweetie, I'm right behind you. Make sure your phone is always on."

"But I don't see you."

My heart dropped. I swallowed hard.

"No, no. I'm still in California. I'm boarding a flight and I should be in Dallas in a few hours. When your plane lands, wait for me at the airport. I'll phone you when I get there."

"All right, I'll . . . wait for your call."

But she didn't ask me why I was meeting her in Dallas, which was disturbing.

Once I arrived in Dallas and met up with her at the airport, we rushed to my doctor—a general practitioner. He examined her but could not find anything physically wrong. I explained how she was acting out strange behavior and was intensely sensitive. She would cry for no reason and lose her sense of timing. He told us to go straight to the Emergency Room immediately.

## Waiting, Hoping, Fearing

We rushed to the nearest hospital. As usual, the emergency department was crowded and the anticipated wait time added to my anxiety. Pat was generally calm about the situation. We stood before the nurse's station to register and she began a series of questions to grade the urgency of our case.

"Any major life changes?"

I said, "My doctor told us to rush here. It's an emergency."

The nurse continued with the triage process, citing a standard script. It was her job, but for us, it was aggravating. I knew the drill, but it was frustrating to prove it was a real emergency. What's an "emergency" anyway? It's a matter of perception. I sensed the nurse was misreading our situation from the outset. We had to pitch a good story to convince her it was an emergency. But we failed to do so and I could hardly suppress my displeasure. The nurse remained apathetic. She was steadfast in doing her job as a triage nurse. All the while, Pas was in a state of bewilderment showing little emotions.

In response to the nurse's question, I said, "The only thing I can think of is I've been away in California."

The nurse immediately looked up, gave me a probing glance and said, "I see." Then she jotted a note in the log. At that moment, I knew my answer had created a problem. In my experience as an ambulance driver in high school, I could understand the nurse's perspective, but it only exacerbated the issue. We were in a "catch-22" situation. When she heard I was away in California, I suspected she ranked us low on the priority list, maybe behind the least sick person in the waiting room.

Based on the nurse's words and cavalier attitude, I viewed her decision as a false verdict. I became livid when I thought her face showed signs of repulsion towards me. I had no control over the situation and I was ready to explode with frustration. We could only hope and pray.

The nurse directed us to take a seat. People waiting sneezed or coughed with runny noses and others casually read magazines and chatted. A teenager was munching on a putrid-smelling hamburger, sipping a soda. In comparison, none were as critical as Pat—*non-threatening ailments, hardly emergencies.* As the minutes clicked by, my frustration turned to anger.

After waiting forty-five minutes, they finally put us in an examination room. Then we waited another fifteen minutes before the doctor arrived. The doctor came in and introduced herself. In her middle 30s, she had short blonde hair, a turned-up nose and a haughty attitude. I explained the events at the airport and how we had just seen our doctor in detail. Pat had no physical evidence of symptoms. Only her disorientation, a cloud over her usual sunny disposition, losing track of time and having headaches.

The ER doctor's presumptive, arrogant approach surprised me. She asked her questions tersely, acting as if she was dealing with a routine, minor issue. I suspected the triage nurse's notes may have had a bearing on her attitude. I felt a pang of guilt. Maybe this wouldn't have happened if I had stayed in Dallas.

Making matters worse, the underlying feelings of remorse were recurrent: I was complicit in separating Pat from her family. I felt repentant about how she had left her home in the U.K. to marry me. Self-imposed guilt was an ever-present dark cloud that had subconsciously built up over the years. Perhaps this onset of remorse was partly because of my religious upbringing—a deep-seated phenomenon within my heart and soul. Though we had created a beautiful family and had a happy marriage, the fact that Pat had left her homeland and family plagued me with nagging self-reproach.

On the other hand, our relationship grew stronger over the years, unlike some marriages. And I'm sure her family were proud of us. It was an unspoken phenomenon, a deep feeling of romantic love, a connection, an emotional bond. When times were tough, it took grit to overcome, maintain the relationship and continue a happy marriage. Our love enabled us to persevere. As intimated in scripture, husband and wife should celebrate their love in behavior and sensuality and we adhered to that principle, the glue that holds marriages together.

Our deep sense of oneness now had us anxiously together, physically and spiritually, waiting in the ER for a diagnosis. It was a tragic dilemma, an incredible twilight moment. Her fate was my fate.

A nurse came into the room and abruptly interrupted our conversation with the ER doctor. The doctor turned to us and said, "I have to check on a patient. I'll be back." I gritted my teeth.

The doctor returned ten minutes later; she said, "I'll have to run some tests — an MRI — to help find the problem." Pat and the doctor left the room. I waited anxiously, worrying about Pat's bizarre condition. I had no idea what it could be and the minutes seemed like hours.

## Grim News

After another half-hour of stressful waiting, her attitude was markedly different when the doctor finally returned. Her face was solemn and her eyes compassionate—she seemed more humane than she had before, more approachable.

"What is it?" I asked, my voice tight, my body braced.

"We found a tumor, . . . a brain tumor."

I was speechless. With barely any warning, reality had slammed us hard in the gut. I gasped, took a deep breath and slowly exhaled. The doctor's voice echoed clear, but I didn't want to hear the words or accept her message.

*A tumor?* The words felt like dozens of poisoned arrows had penetrated my heart. I went numb, became light-headed, then took another deep breath and leaned against the wall.

I uttered, "A tumor?"

The doctor looked at me with compassion, her attitude consoling. She slowly nodded. "Yes."

"You mean, . . . cancer?" I could hardly get the dreaded word out. *No, no, not my Pat!*

The doctor added in a nearly inaudible tone, "Not certain it's malignant but likely." Her words were like daggers piercing me. I raised my eyes to the ceiling. *"God, please don't let this be true!"* I felt the moment sucking the life out of me and I struggled to hold back tears.

I looked at Pat. All the while, her face was unemotional. She remained silent, seemingly shielded from the horror, oblivious to it all. Then, when she turned to me, I could see it in her eyes. She realized she was in some danger but was unaware of the seriousness.

My heart dropped. I wanted to act brave, unalarmed, but a gripping sensation of impending doom and sorrow overwhelmed me. I tried to keep a poker face, but couldn't hold back tears. I held Pat in my arms and squeezed her tight.

If only I had not gone to California and stayed in Dallas. If only, if only. I didn't know what or who else to blame—and if only it were a matter of blame. I came to realize all the "ifs" wouldn't have made a difference. We had been apart several times before and there had never been any problems. Who has ultimate control over life situations? Only God the Almighty. But being philosophical didn't help; an enormous weight continued to spread across my shoulders.

We were at a catastrophic juncture. I faced reality and tried to maintain hope over depression, sanity over mania. And I refused to surrender to despair. Moments of dread came and went, but I convinced myself to foster some resilience and optimism, keeping my wits and set to move forward with courage rather than fear.

# Chapter Twenty

## Beyond Desolation

F lash forward to the present, on the way to the beach house on Crystal Beach. It's a Friday morning in December, and the drive is going smoothly. I hit green lights most of the way through Galveston on Broadway Avenue. Traffic at the ferry landing is sparse and the wait is short. There is a chill in the air at 45 degrees and 20-knot winds out of the southeast. At the edge of the dock, the Lone Star flag flies straight and flat like a weather vane and a drizzle covers my windshield with glittering droplets. Birds circle the ferry landing and, in the distance, I see a gaggle of dolphins playfully oscillating, poking their fins just above the choppy ship channel.

Before long, the ferry "John W. Johnson" will be easing into the landing dock. An LED sign over the entrance flashes "MARSEC Level 1", which is the Maritime Security Level for security measures in effect. In this day and age, security is at the forefront. Vehicles can be searched at random and justifiably so. Nowadays, we are vulnerable to many threats. And the Texas coast has an abundance of maritime vessels, oil, gas and chemical refineries, all of which demand the strictest of security.

I pull up in line on the ferry, shut down my rumbling diesel engine and set the brake on my trusty Dodge pickup. My mind regresses and meanders far back through the channels of memory. I don't recall security being such an urgent matter, but times have changed in many ways. In our days in the 50s, we were seldom interrupted just for security reasons. My late-night, early-morning ambulance trips from Port Arthur to the University of Texas Medical Branch in Galveston—just a mile or so from the ferry landing—were usually routine, non-eventful. Compared to back in the day, Galveston has changed. I remember when the Texas Rangers shut down the rackets in 1957. Before that time, the Rangers raided Galveston, crushed slot machines and dumped them into the bay and grinded up dice tables. Then there was the devastation of the city by Hurricane Carla in 1961. Today, Galveston seems little more than a glimmer of its colorful, historically rich past.

As the ship turned northeast, I saw a familiar landmark: the jet-black, iconic Bolivar Point Lighthouse jutting from the ground like a giant needle. Then I turn and look northward, where a line of refinery smokestacks in Texas City silhouettes the hazy blue horizon. Then in a few minutes, we pass Seawolf Park on Pelican Island, a memorial to the dry-docked USS Seawolf, a U.S. naval submarine accidentally sunk by our Navy in World War II. The Park offers fishing piers and the Galveston Naval Museum, where you can tour the submarine and learn about military history.

The ferry trip is 2.7 miles across the channel and it takes an average of 18 minutes. The basin is without large tankers but several tugboats guiding barges through relatively calm waters. Invariably, flocks of seafowls flutter around the docks hunting food and perch on the ferry for a ride to the other side.

I'm at the beach house now, gazing out the second-floor back window at a turquoise blue, misty sky over a constellation of colorful beach homes. A thin veneer of rainwater shines on cement foundations that support lodgings resting on high pilings. A hazy, sprinkled horizon is above a foamy, salt-water surf washing the empty beach towards the south. Like a wheel of fortune, my mind spins with memories—the fun of growing up in the 40s and 50s, joining the military, going to Europe, meeting Pat and our remarkable courtship, getting married, working in Asia, traveling and having two beautiful children.

Then the spinning wheel abruptly stops at the most traumatic point of losing Pat.

* * *

After his examination, the doctor uttered, "glioblastoma multiforme." The phrase was like a bomb exploding in my ears. Just the sound of it meant something terrible.

He added, "It's a rare, aggressive type of cancer that normally attacks young, bright people."

My heart missed a few beats. *Why Pat?* I could hardly believe what I heard. It didn't make sense; why was such a wholesome person like Pat going through this? There were no answers, just spiritual disillusionment. I thought God would take me first, not the other way around.

We pursued every option throughout the ordeal of multiple examinations, prognoses and treatment. I would do anything to rid Pat of the persistent enemy. Finally, we reluctantly agreed to surgery – removing the tumor. It was a gruesome thought, but it was the only viable alternative.

When Pat came out of the operating room, I could hardly hold back tears. The sight of her head wrapped in gauze was heartbreaking. A gush of sorrow and despair enveloped me. Making matters worse, I recalled scenes of her in the hospital bed in England after her car accident. Grieving had begun well before her death and I learned to cope. At least well enough to struggle through a daily routine. Still, to witness your loved one in these predicaments is devastating, physically and mentally. When not at work and staying with Pat at the Richardson hospital, I would go to the chapel and pray. Lacking proper sleep, I would also stretch out on the floor and take naps.

She went into rehabilitation after recovery. Even throughout this nightmare, Pat maintained her uplifting attitude with her magnetic personality. True to form, she made friends quickly and played the comic. It humbled me to see her strength and her will to ignore her plight and enjoy the people around her. Meanwhile, I moved into a ground-floor apartment so she could come home in a wheelchair. I hired two caregivers for round-the-clock services. We used the last days to spend time together out by the pool, chatting away. Pat's vibrant personality was still intact, but physically, things got worse. Within a few months, we had to call in hospice care.

Pat lay in the hospital-type bed in our bedroom, surrounded by a bereaving family, Peter, Angela and her husband Steve, including Pat's sister Jackie and her husband, John. I sat at her bedside, with my head next to hers on the pillow. I heard her breathing fade, then slowed to her very last breath. Pat joined God in heaven.

It was an emotionally exhausting moment. I repeatedly told myself Pat was with God in hopes of some relief. But relief never came. The trauma of it tightly wrapped my heart in a perpetual straight-jacket.

We arranged funeral proceedings, including cremation. First, we had a memorial service at the funeral home where a small gathering of family and friends attended. Then we had services at All Saints Catholic Church in Dallas and a favorite priest, Father Paul, presided. Many people were in attendance, including a team of buddies from the local 1st Marine Division Association. My niece Kristen and my friend Lloyd and his wife Anne read scriptures. Other friends narrated their short, typically funny stories about Pat, refreshing at first but a sad afterthought. Some of it is still a numbing blur to me. I can't thoroughly explain how I felt when it was over and everyone had left, perhaps like falling off a cliff and in vertigo. My world was turning upside down.

I remember a deep vacuum, emptiness, being lonely for Pat, begrudging her demise, and feeling intense sorrow. My universe was a haze of darkness. I often visited the chapel to seek God's guidance to understand and have faith in His loving protection. All the while, mourning, sadness, and confusion were a distraction. My equilibrium was out of kilter with any life ambitions. It is unfathomable how grief affects memories, at least with mine. There are some blank spots, perhaps subconsciously suppressed.

Her ashes rest in a place similar to the tranquil pier at the marina in Emeryville and the serene levee in Port Arthur. Her ashes are permanently interned in Dallas, outside on the perimeter of a mausoleum. The urn vault is about eight feet from a pond. A perpetual waterspout sprays mist across placidly waving water with floating white lilies. The traffic buzz from a nearby freeway added variety to the ambiance, reminiscent of our colorful, dynamic lives together. Pat was full of life, a vibrant life, and I cherish having been together in several major cities in the world—memories of such an energetic, loving person, no matter where we were. I can't think of a better place for her to rest. Inscribed on the internment chamber is her date of birth and death and my name and birthdate are below.

I pushed the occurrence into a closet for a long time, in remote corners of my mind. I was grieving, but I countered with work, throwing myself into my job. I tried to prevent my guilt-ridden dream story from disrupting day-to-day life. I'd recover from those sleepless nights during lunch hours when I would nap in my car in the parking lot. Eventually, I came to realize self-awareness had shut down at the point of acute trauma. The trauma morphed into a cocoon, with me inside as I underwent the stages of mourning. The loss of Pat severed my heart and soul, and I made an effort to encapsulate and cling to the memories of times we shared. But without Pat at my side, the memories amounted to little more than an empty bottle.

Grieving has no perceivable end goal. You wonder how and if you'll ever burst out of the cocoon, regain psychological and emotional traction and balance again. There's no way around it; however, if you're a believer, you're never alone in your demise, spiritually and physically. I especially thanked God for Peter and Angela. They were tremendous support, stabilizing anchors throughout the crisis. I shudder to think of how our loss affected them. I prayed they weren't having grief dreams like mine and could continue a steady course in pursuit of vast potential in life. Thankfully, by all indications, it has proven as such.

The dreams I had then were extraordinary and I kept them secret for a long while. Until now, I only told one person, a professor at a local college and a Christian hands healer. She analyzed the dream story and shared logical answers to "why"? Denial, survivor guilt, refusal to let it go. Her analysis and the sessions helped restore the power of faith and energy. I should have talked to a professional long before that point. With certainty, praying to God and talking and writing about grief is a cathartic release, a stimulus for healing and solace.

Although, on occasion, I thought my mysterious dreams weren't merely nightmares. They were convincing hallucinations — realistic, believable enough to ring true, even in wakening hours.

# Chapter Twenty-One

## Dark Dreams

*This world is but a canvas to our imagination.*
*—Henry David Thoreau*

Pellets of sweat covered my body. Night after night, the dark dream story profoundly infused my subconscious with false hope, then heavy letdowns. Soul-stirring grief had infected my psyche, my sense of balance, my universe. Tormenting bouts of floundering, flailing and ripping blankets away left me exhausted. Sometimes I felt imaginary shock waves dashing through my veins, awakening me in a fluster. With little sleep, mustering the energy to work was challenging by morning. It took a heavy dose of caffeine to keep awake well enough to navigate Dallas traffic, get to the office and effectively do my job. I also tried diversionary tactics to embrace a healthy life by socializing more with friends. But the intrusive dream story lingered in my mind. All along, I never discussed my condition with anyone—even my children.

Grieving has no boundaries and timing is variable. It had been some three years since Pat's passing and I continued to have weird dreams. I had one foot in the physical world and the other in a bizarre dream world. I understand dreams supposedly echo real-life scenarios. But for me, it was the other way around: the dream story carried over into the real world. In my dream world, I falsely convinced myself she was still here somewhere on this planet, constantly eluding me in an inexplicable game of hide-and-seek. I was trapped in something almost like a perpetual psychedelic state—not drug-induced but brought on by dream-related visions that overlapped wakefulness. Subconsciously, I rejected Pat's passing. I wanted her alive, back with me, enjoying happy times again. The dreams offered that false possibility—and wanting so badly for it to be true left me living in two different worlds.

My brain played cognitive tricks, leaving me hanging, often unable to discern what was real and what was not. Thoughts and feelings carried over from the dream story to the real world. The two meshed together, making them more intense and more dramatic. Imagine a chronological film that only plays at night, logically formatted with a plot, crisis, discovery and change. It was an absurd film with episodes, a mini-series with a cast of only two characters: Pat and me. The set, site and scenery changed, but the theme remained unchanged. Memories exist in an environment affected by persistent changes and emotions that may transform our thinking and recollections. When you dredge up the past, your feelings override and some factual details may fall by the wayside. Reminiscence is a complex process and a monkey-wrench thrown into the mix may skew the facts, reforming inaccurate information.

To understand what was happening to me I briefly researched the subjects of lucid dreaming and narcolepsy. The dreamer is consciously aware in a lucid dream, controlling the dream story. But in my case, lucid dreaming wasn't likely, since I had little control over dream events. Narcolepsy, on the other hand, is a condition where the person is caught between a perpetual dream world and the waking world, going from one to the other, not feeling fully asleep and rarely feeling fully awake.

I believe my experiences also included something called "bereavement hallucinations" (BH) or "sensory hallucinations." Based on a study published in 2015, this common condition can occur with upwards of 60% of widowed people within ten years of losing a mate. BH is perceived as communication with or sensing the presence of the deceased. In a report in 2013, up to 80% of bereaved people may have had this experience at least once. I'm not suggesting the physical presence and verbal communications with Pat were actual; they were simply a reflection of my passionate and powerful hopes—vivid impressions in my conscious and subconscious worlds—within the realm of normal for people in my situation.

In retrospect and whatever the scientific terminology, I was grappling with recovery and, at the same time, experiencing convoluted stages of grief—shock, disorder and bewilderment. Some generically call it "closure," but at the time and even now, natural closure was elusive, distant, out of reach. It was challenging and painful to go through life on a steady course; my course was an erratic, helplessly emotional journey on a bumpy, meandering road without a compass or steering wheel. I believed my condition was unique and that no one else would understand what I was going through. I thought that, given enough time, my situation would complete its entire progression and I would be back to normalcy.

I didn't know what help I needed except to make some sense of it all. Part of me knew Pat was no longer here but in a heavenly place. Another factor was in denial and continued to play out the dream scenario. Sometimes I would light a candle, focus on the flame and go into a meditative state of consciousness. It was an attempt to understand what was happening in my dreams and help me get back to living in the real world. I had to deal with my subconscious to dispel the dream effects, which seemed to override rational consciousness, keeping me in a constant battle, an unresolvable conflict. On occasion, I became irrational, helplessly clinging to the impossible expectation that she would return to me in life. Then a mountain of frustration would come crashing down. *"Face reality,"* I would tell myself; "we're all mortals. She cannot return to me, and I can no longer have her presence and witness her scintillating personality. I'll have to learn to live without her." But try as I might, the serial dream story persisted.

The puzzling yet realistic imaginings went on and on in a spiral. The heartache, the pain, the deep heaviness often threw me into a swirling, dark abyss, eliciting nagging onsets of sadness. I could function reasonably normally during my waking hours, but the effects of shock, overwrought feelings and recovery would often clash, resulting in confusion and stress. I would feel miserable one minute, overcome with grief the next and then for whatever reason, suddenly feel inspired with merriment. It was peculiar and disheartening. I began to wonder if I would ever overcome this phenomenon.

I recently dreamed about a scene in Pat's hometown—an example of dreams reflecting the thoughts and emotions of a real-life episode. It was an uplifting, serene dream. When I awoke, it resulted in a melancholy mood that demonstrated my longing for years gone by—those happy days of courting Pat, socializing with her family and enjoying the quaint environment and hospitality of a small town in England. I reminisce about those times quite often. I must, however, remind myself that it happened over a half-century ago when we were young, with fewer responsibilities, abounding with energy and excitement for the future. But I wasn't in that world anymore. I was in no man's land.

I felt trapped in a mental prison with no windows, no doors, only rigid concrete walls My condition felt claustrophobic, like real-life solitary confinement adding to my already intense anxiety. It seemed impossible to break out of this years-long dream world, but eventually, I convinced myself to fight it off, put it all behind me and develop an iron will to survive. The dreams would subsequently subside, though not in their entirety. Some details would slowly fade, but the traumatic scars are forever carved in my mind, my soul.

In the opening scene of the core dream, I was alone in our bedroom. I opened the doors of our closet. Pat's clothes were missing. Next, I went into the bathroom. None of her toiletries were there. I searched all over the house and couldn't find any of her things. She had suddenly vanished, flat-out disappeared, without a warning or clue—not even a note. I went numb with puzzlement, plagued with a void that broke my heart and pierced my soul. She had packed her belongings and left without a goodbye—no note, no notice and no clues. I had no idea why she left, where she had gone or whether she would return.

My world had spun out of control, wobbling like a spinning top, then tipping to the floor, motionless. Sometimes even in waking hours, it was difficult to focus on the simplest chores. My ambition transformed into near bleakness.

I investigated every avenue to find Pat without success in the next series of dream scenes. After several weeks of nights studying the nightmare search scenes, I dreamed that I had finally discovered where she might be and then her tracked down. She was in a remote, unrecognizable location—the type of nondescript, illogical place that can only appear in dreams. I must've found an address somehow because I recall sending a written message that said in part, "Why did you leave me?" In the note, I pleaded with her to meet me and talk face-to-face about what was happening. "Please, let's talk this over. I can't live without you."

For me, it was an exceedingly sorrowful, depressive dream sequence, partly because, in some strange way, I was culpable. We'd had a happy life together, but relationships are not perfect and I wanted to make amends for any hurt I'd caused Pat. If only she came home, I would make things better, in whatever terms she wanted. But she was steadfast in her decision. I persisted, pleading for another chance.

"Please, let's start over."

She hesitated for a moment and said, "I'll think about it." Her words flooded my heart with excitement at the chance of being together again. Before we parted, I convinced Pat to meet me at a restaurant to discuss the situation further.

It's vague, but I can still visualize our rendezvous. We met in an old-fashioned diner. The booths had chrome-adorned retro tables, shiny red-and-white puffy vinyl seats and miniature tableside jukebox song selectors. It was mid-morning and we were having a continental breakfast—warm butter croissants, jam, fruit and coffee. Hopefully, this reunion will be the road to redemption.

Pat sat across the Formica-top table. I slid a quarter in the jukebox selector slot and punched the button for *I Only Have Eyes for You* by the *Flamingos*. The song started playing on the vintage Wurlitzer jukebox across the room. As I gazed into her eyes, my eagerness reached a peak of confidence that we would soon be back together again. I was elated.

My mind swirled with a host of questions, but as it turned out, I stumbled through a convoluted conversation, grasping at straws, trying to find answers. Some of it made no sense at all. Why she had gone away was still a mystery I was desperate to solve.

"Please tell me, why did you leave me?"

Pat continually changed the subject and evaded the issue. Her responses left me feeling like I was in a strait-jacket that got tighter and tighter. At this point, the dream always became fuzzy. I could only presume she was unhappy because I had erred in my ways; I must have done something to upset her. The dialogue between us then became very ambiguous, tense and traumatic at the same time. I felt an enormous guilt trip, like a wrecking ball demolishing me. I expressed remorse, asking for another meeting to talk it over.

"We'll meet again. It'll be all right."

I was euphoric, filled with confidence.

## Tarnished Jewels in the Dream Box

Some dreams were lovely and enchanting. A sweet dream scene that occasionally occupied my sleep was this: We were on the Intracoastal levee in Port Arthur, sitting on a green and white checkered blanket, a picnic basket at our side. We quietly basked in the sun with a gentle, moist breeze from the Gulf whisking our faces. A cluster of wide-spanning stratocumulus clouds slowly drifted overhead. The sun intermittently dimmed as the clouds hid its face. Then sun rays broke through and fanned out like fingers, shining upon us—a touch of God's warm healing powers. These are moments to cherish, another jewel in the box.

And in my dreams, I reviewed the times we had driven to the draw-bridge at the canal, joining a line of cars waiting for ships passing through to refineries in Port Neches. Above, the moonlit sky was clear, dotted with twinkling stars. The Pleasure Island lights shimmered on the tranquil canal. Like a fresh flower in the spring, Pat's scent drifted in the air and it was an opportune time to cuddle.

Over the bridge, on the other side of the canal, we cruised down Seawall Boulevard towards the entertainment center and the Lake Sabine levee. Stair-stepped granite blocks rimmed the lake, forming a romantic alcove. We parked at the far end, near the Pleasure Pier Ballroom.

"Look at the moon," Pat said in the dream, a serene expression on her face. "It ripples off the waves and shines on us." Under a diamond-studded sky, we could see parked cars, misty windows hiding lovers inside, moonlight reflecting off chrome and windshields. The sultry Gulf breeze whispered through the palm trees, enhancing the natural, pleasant ambiance of the setting. The Lake Sabine tide splashed against the seawall, spraying our windshield with glistening teardrops of saltwater. An old favorite song from the 1950s, *The Sea of Love* by Phil Phillips, echoed from the car's radio. We sat and talked about our plans for the wedding and starting anew in Washington, D.C.

Then the dream fizzled into a dark chasm, the end of a pleasant segment in the dream story.

Our next dream meeting was more upbeat. I persuaded Pat to return home and start over again. She agreed to give it another chance. We were together—a fresh new day, a new life on the horizon. In my dream, as in our actual relationship, life was fun, exciting and passionate, reminiscent of the happy early days in London.

But this beautiful dream phase was short-lived. Little by little, my dream visions of Pat faded away. Much like the night decades earlier, at the Corby train platform, when I watched her slowly disappear into the snow-filled darkness, deep drifts at her feet. As she stood beside the tracks, my dazzling star had gradually dimmed and vanished in the swirling blanket of floating snowflakes.

That memory can open a faucet of tears.

*The goodbye was grim*
*We'd been together, bonded as one*
*Hold steadfast my love; you are my glim*
*Forever connected, our reunion will be done*

# Chapter Twenty-Two

## Reality - Losses Multiply

Since losing Pat, I've also lost several loved ones and friends. Too many to mention more than a few here. It's lonely without them, but it is an inevitable part of life. I learned this many years ago, during my ambulance service days and specifically after losing my cousin L.J. Tatman in a tragic motorcycle accident. Married with three children, L.J. was only in his early twenties.

Many of my family, friends and classmates have passed.

My good friend Bo Guilbeau retired from his dental practice a few years ago. Shortly afterward, due to a longtime respiratory issue, he passed away from complications at 77. I was with him a few days before he left us and we watched a favorite movie, "A Fish Called Wanda." That viewing reminded us of our type of youthful antics and pranks, which resulted in loads of laughter. Just days later, he was gone from this life. And his brother "Snake" recently died unexpectedly of Leukemia.

Decades before that, our compadre Mikey, a professional accountant, died of heart failure. He had had heart bypass surgery several years before, but he gave out while playing tennis at 36. The quintessential prankster dropped to the court floor motionless, the big Texas sun shining upon him. His fellow players thought it was another prank but quickly realized it wasn't.

## Coping Mechanisms

As far as I know, Pat had no enemies. By chance, if someone were unfriendly it would have been their problem, not Pat's. She didn't have a vindictive bone in her body. Although, she could be a formidable opponent fending for righteousness—a trait most people respect.

My battle was and still is coping with grief, the archenemy of anyone who has lost a loved one. Some say the process of grieving has five phases: denial, anger, bargaining, depression and acceptance. There are other opinions of the process, but it's all the same: I think it was suffering from losing a loved one and I was entering into unchartered waters. It's been extraordinary for me, as it will be for most. There are no clear-cut lines and everyone reacts in their way. Some are extroverts about grief who rely on support groups like family, friends, etc. Others take a completely different turn in life, embarking on an adventure, a change in lifestyle, or a distraction. And some, like me, or more introverted about it. We keep our feelings private and deal with grief inwardly but remain vulnerable to the five phases mentioned above. There was no anger involved when I lost Pat—just deep pain and sorrow and perhaps a tad of denial evidenced by misery and my dream episodes. And yet, I could do nothing about her illness; it was an incurable disease. Maybe a little bargaining crept in as I fought the depression part. We were looking forward to more years together.

My primary coping strategy was a form of auto-suggestion—convincing myself to accept the facts, keep my feet on the ground and move forward in life. Applying logical thought processes, I told myself to think, feel and behave honorably. Perhaps God was shining His guiding light during the exercise. He knew my world was emotionally chaotic, spinning out of control. I was in a funk and for a while, I acted a bit crazy, careless, out of character, which is common based on others in the same predicament. Like vertigo, the emotional disorientation caused by grief will skew a person's thinking and cause erroneous reactions. Again, I think with the prompting of God's direction, I was able to overcome craziness by continually recalling my life verse:

> *In all thy ways, acknowledge Him.*
> *And He shall direct thy paths.*
> —Proverbs 3:6 King James Version (KJV)

God directed me to a practice I've used in the past. And if done right, auto-suggestion is more effective, safer than medications and with no risk of drug addiction. Auto-suggestion is not necessarily self-hypnosis, but pretty close to it. It's a technique, similar to the placebo effect that impresses one's thinking and brings guidance according to verbalized suggestions of feelings, behavior or personal goals.

As an aviator, I know that feelings and emotions have no place in the cockpit of an aircraft; they can lead to loss of control, resulting in a deadly tailspin. In that predicament, the only hope, other than an act of God, is using the plane's instruments. Trusting one's feelings will usually lead to disaster. There's a way to correct the behavior of a spinning airplane and regain control, but it will go against one's innate feelings. A good pilot knows enough to ignore feelings and rely on the instruments.

I came to realize it was the same with my situation. The kind of pain that accompanies grief over the loss of a loved one can put a person's life in what pilots call a "graveyard spin"—swirling chaos of depression and hopelessness—a natural reaction to losing a loved one, which can lead to suicide. I chose to ignore negative emotions rely on spiritual instruments and logic. Eventually, my choice paid off; I was able to pull my life out of the dream tailspin without crashing.

## Keeping the Faith

*And not only so, but we glory in tribulations also:*
*knowing that tribulation worketh patience;*
*And patience, experience; and experience, hope.*
—Romans 5:3-4 King James Version (KJV)

Surviving the loss of a loved one can be a long, arduous process, one of the most traumatic experiences in life and one that requires patience and hope. But what are the practical methods? I thank God for my time with her and for helping me through my grievance.

Besides faith, I would occasionally light a single candle, focus on it and repeat a logical mantra either verbally or mentally. It was a time of close connection with God, a sort of telepathic communication, including a favorite prayer:

*Oh Christ Jesus, when all is darkness*
*and we feel our weakness and helplessness,*
*give us the sense of Your presence,*
*Your love, and Your strength.*
*Help us to have perfect trust*
*in Your protecting love*
*and strengthening power,*
*so that nothing may frighten or worry us,*
*for, living close to You,*
*we shall see Your hand,*
*Your purpose, Your will through all things.*
—Saint Ignatius of Loyola

I believe these practices encouraged me to overcome, undoubtedly an influence from God. The subconscious mind accepts the suggestive statements. After repeatedly telling myself how to think, feel and behave, I was on a path to surviving grief. Even so, I sometimes became remiss, discouraged and failed in the process. I hate thinking about that part. And my behavior was not always virtuous. But my most prevalent mistake was not talking to anyone about my dreams. Talking it over with someone—preferably a professional—offers a remedial effect, treatment, a release of pressure and relief from the thought of fighting the battle alone.

Grief is a complicated phenomenon and there is no "right" way of dealing with the loss of loved ones. It depends on the survivor, the person who must endure and carry on with life. One helpful thing I learned is to focus on how the deceased lived instead of how they died. Together with social and physical activities, positive memories are an antidote to depression. Also, maintaining a balanced diet, good health, and especially exercise are critical factors for mental health. Exercise relieves stress by releasing endorphins, which counteract emotional and physical pain. Endorphins also release other chemicals, such as dopamine, serotonin and oxytocin. These neurotransmitters are the "happy chemicals" that trigger a positive mood.

I'm mulling over my dreadful grief experience. Naively, I did not seek professional help during the stages of grievance: shock, disconnection, confusion and emptiness—a mountain of trauma. After a happy life together and losing Pat, my center of gravity spun out of control. During short periods of sleep, I first dreamed of the distressing events details of her sickness and death. Then it was a dream story of denial. My counteraction was praying the rosary with a group at church, which was beneficial in many ways. Albeit temporary, I felt some relief, comfort, belonging and reintegration into the real world. Looking around the chapel, I felt compassion for people in the group, which was therapeutic in effect. But the bizarre dreams persisted and I wondered if it was a unique phenomenon. I was relieved to learn they are considered a common form of grief.

There are studies about "visitation dreams" of the bereaved, whereby the deceased appear in dreams and give a message of some sort, such as words of comfort or advice to the bereaved. I find it interesting that the deceased often appeared young and healthy in these dreams, which encouraged grievers to believe there is life after death. In my case, I was in a state of denial and not sure I had visitation dreams. I was experiencing lucid, realistic, but uncontrollable dreams—a heart-breaking roller-coaster series of encouragements and letdowns, a futile effort to bring Pat and me back together again. Amid moments of optimism in my waking hours—derived from joyous scenes in the dreams—emotional chaos interfered. I cherished the positives, blending them into my waking world. It helped me build a new life, and it was a matter of waiting for the dreams to subside. In time, they did, but a degree of grief lingers.

About two years after Pat's death, the illusions slowly faded; reality started to overshadow the dream episodes. I'm not too surprised about the length of time it took for the delusions to begin to dissipate. We had been together for over 40 years and it was difficult to "move on" without her. I still have fond, loving memories of her. I try to dwell on the happy times and from a selfish viewpoint, I can't help but think of what I had and what I lost. Of course, I still have our family—Peter and Angela, our grandson Gavin and all the rest. Invariably, the enduring effects are challenging. We all suffer from a tremendous loss.

I believe grieving never ends; it only becomes less intense. Resilience, tenacity and controlled movement through the stages help ease the pain. Over time, I learned how to tolerate the effects of grief. As some people advise, it's impossible to ever "get over" the loss of a loved one. I reject that remark, but I admit there is some merit to living out the rest of one's life in a resolve to move past the pain and get on with life.

People use the term "closure," but I think that's a misnomer. There can never be closure, only a state of resolution and a sliver of peace of mind.

Most importantly, I learned to give myself a break from guilt. Guilt can only harm. Thinking negatively about oneself creates a downward spiral into more negative thoughts and feelings, whether justifiable or not. I had to live with myself for the rest of my life, and respecting myself was the first step toward loving and respecting others—a vital tenet of life. Losing a deeply loved one—a relationship built on solid rock—can be the most significant loss of a lifetime. But it doesn't have to mean giving up on life; you can and should—*must*—love and respect yourself and others. In fact, contrary to logic, losing someone we deeply love can help us become more loving toward others.

To reference a biblical passage, ". . . love your neighbor as yourself." (Matthew 22:39); some interpret this as, *"You must love yourself before you can truly love others."* Either way, Pat was the perfect example of this truth. She's with God now and I hear her message from heaven:

*We are as we were. I am not dead*
*My spirit is alive in the sun, in the air*
*We will always be a pair*
*When birds sing and music is in your head*
*We are as we were. I am not dead.*

# Epilogue

## Reflections

S ome twenty years after Pat's death, I'm sitting on the sun deck at the beach house, head tilted back, gazing at the blue sky and listening to the gently rolling waves. The floating cotton-ball clouds overhead and a steady breeze open my mind to a broad perception of the past. The atmosphere triggers a recollection of my life—a reflective totality of life events in chronological order. As noted in this book, some events emerge in great detail and others fall by the wayside. The act of reviewing my past helps me know where I've been, where I am and how to move forward. I've learned to be more patient and content and better weather the storms of pain and heartache, such as Pat's death. I cherish romantic moments Pat and I had, like picnics on the levee and simply private time together. I'm enormously lucky and grateful that we were blessed to share our lives.

Overall, I've realized by the grace of God, I've lived a good, whole and colorful life!

Having Pat in my life for roughly forty years was the most significant part. They were the happiest years, full of variety and I cherish the memories. Her positive influence on my life is permanent and invaluable. We had a remarkable courtship in the U.K. and beyond that, we experienced different cultures and made many friends throughout our relationship. Together we accomplished many things, including traveling, performing music, living in several places in the U.S. and the world and having two beautiful children. Our time together was fulfilling and often enchanting—a collage of dazzling brush strokes on my canvas of life.

Here's a thumbnail sketch of my life from my perspective at a ripe old age. Before meeting Pat, I was fortunate to have grown up during the "happy days" era of the 40s and 50s. At eighteen, I joined the elite U.S. Marine Corps and earned my first stripe while in the Infantry Training Regiment. After being posted at the First Missile Battalion in Twenty-Nine Palms, California, I qualified for Embassy Guard duty in London, where I met Pat. Soon after my four-year tour in the Marines, we married. Over the next few years, we had Peter and Angela while living in the Washington, D.C., area. I attended college at night and worked full-time during the day. After a stint as a government contractor in the Vietnam war, I established a business franchise in Bangkok, Thailand. After that, we settled in Dallas, where I continued a career in the IT industry, working for several major companies. I eventually started up a successful computer firm. After selling the business, I continued as an IT consultant, working on contracts with several major corporations.

These days, I stay occupied with business consulting, music, writing and keeping in touch with family and friends. And the beach house is like a sanctuary for meditation and contemplation. Staying active in business is also fulfilling. Or, put another way, providing a product or service in return for a profit requires faith, tenacity and hard work on my part. And success requires all-encompassing teamwork from my workers and clientele. That leads me to relationships, which are, for me, a vital life tenet and an essential component of living a Christian-based life. Spending time with my family and friends is a satisfying activity that keeps the quality of my relationships alive and well. Fellowship, socializing, and maintaining relationships are inspirational therapeutics for my mental health and help me maintain a positive attitude. Besides spending time with my family and friends, I also go to the local YMCA gym for physical fitness and socializing. I also play the drums in a church band on weekends, giving me a feeling of worshipful service.

Occasionally, I'll fly a small airplane (with a safety pilot) to prove I can still handle it and to savor the peacefulness of clean air, the blue sky and the clouds. Like the beach house scenario, flying is a source of calmness and serenity. There's a saying attributed to Leonardo da Vinci:

> *"When once you have tasted flight, you will walk the earth with your eyes turned skyward, for there you have been and there you will long to return."*

Flight is not only comforting; it is incredibly empowering. When I'm at an altitude of, say, ten thousand feet between clear blue skies above and a layer of clouds below, I feel closer to God in heaven.

> *For the Lord Himself will descend from heaven with a shout, with the voice of the archangel and with the trumpet of God, and the dead in Christ will rise first. Then we who are alive, who remain, will be caught up together with them in the clouds to meet the Lord in the air, and so we will always be with the Lord.*
> — 1 Thessalonians 4:16-17 – (NASB)

The joy of writing is unending. For most writers, it's a means of catharsis, a word that stems from the Greek word *kathairein*, which means "cleanse" or "purge." The action of writing effectively purges inner thoughts and emotions and transfers the residue to paper. At times, writing is a relief, a release of worrisome thoughts. By all means, writing is a courageous activity that requires personal humility and vulnerability. And sometimes, it can be downright grueling. It can also be a shining light that brings calmness and peace, improves my mental attitude and helps me understand who I am.

I thank God for protecting my family. Peter, Angela and the rest are healthy and doing well. Peter is still active in his music career and Angela in her real estate business. My grandson Gavin continues to build an impressive career in sports—at this time, he favors basketball.

Everyday life goes on but losing Pat left an indelible, deep scar. Gradually, the crazy dreams became less chaotic and more tolerable. I'm thankful they have diminished. Hanging on to the positive snippets in the dreams during waking hours has helped the healing process and brings an impetus to let go, rejuvenate and enjoy everyday life. Pat's spirit is forever with me, and I have solace in what she said in one of the dreams:

"We'll meet again. It'll be all right."